NATIONAL
GEOGRAPHIC
KiDS

JURASSIC
SMARTS

A JAM-PACKED **FACT BOOK** FOR **DINOSAUR SUPERFANS!**

Jen Agresta +
Stephanie Warren Drimmer

NATIONAL GEOGRAPHIC
WASHINGTON, D.C.

INTRODUCTION

GET READY TO TRAVEL BACK IN TIME TO AN ERA BEFORE HUMANS, WHEN DINOSAURS WALKED THE EARTH! Our planet looked a lot different then than it does now. Places that are now desert were once lush forests, and places that are now icy were warm and bustling with ancient reptiles.

But wait! The time of the dinosaurs—called the Mesozoic era—spanned hundreds of millions of years. During that time, Earth changed a lot. To describe these differences, the Mesozoic is split into three time periods: the Triassic, the Jurassic, and the Cretaceous.

During the Triassic, the earliest of these periods, all the continents on Earth were still connected, forming one giant landmass: Pangaea. The first dinosaurs emerged during this time. By the end of the Cretaceous period, the final days of the dinosaurs (at least, as we usually think of them), Pangaea had split into pieces, forming early versions of the continents we know on Earth today.

This book is called *Jurassic Smarts,* and it's got info about the cool dinos that were around in the Jurassic period. But it's also got info about dinos from the Triassic and the Cretaceous as well. In fact, many of the most popular dinosaurs out there emerged during the Cretaceous!

To learn more about the Mesozoic, turn the page!

Inside this book, you'll find TONS of serious dino stats, but also some silly stuff. Keep an eye out for ...

T. REX SURVIVAL TIPS.

FUN DINOSAUR FACE-OFFS!

CLASS SUPERLATIVES FROM THE DINO HIGH YEARBOOK.

Need a refresh on some important dino terms?
Check out the glossary on page 214.

START HERE.

WHICH

TIME
PERIOD

WOULD YOU LIVE IN?

THE AGE OF DINOSAURS, ALSO CALLED THE MESOZOIC, LASTED FROM 252 TO 66 MILLION YEARS AGO. IT'S DIVIDED UP INTO THREE PERIODS. WHICH WOULD YOU CALL HOME?

WHAT KIND OF CREATURES DO YOU WANT TO SEE?

Show me the dino celebrities!

ARE YOU UP FOR A LITTLE DANGER?

Let's keep it safe.

I'll take a risk!

I'd like to see some lesser known species.

MAMMALS OR DINOSAURS?

Mammals sound fun.

Show me the dinos!

JURASSIC

The Jurassic is your jam. This time period, from 201 to 145 million years ago, was home to giant plant-eaters, stalked by smaller predators like *Ceratosaurus* (p. 50). The first birds rose up in this period as well.

CRETACEOUS

You'd like the Cretaceous, the end of the age of dinosaurs, 145 to 66 million years ago. This period is known for the most famous dinosaurs of all time: from gigantic titanosaurs to hungry hunters like *Velociraptor* to, yep, the *T. rex*. It's also the time when mammals began to spread around the globe.

TRIASSIC

Try out the Triassic. This was the beginning of the Mesozoic, lasting from 252 to 201 million years ago. In this period, known as the dawn of the dinosaurs, you'll see the earliest dinos, such as *Herrerasaurus* (p. 126), roaming Earth.

LITTLE LIMBS

A *CARNOTAURUS* CHASES AFTER *ANTARCTOPELTA*, ITS PREY.

CARNOTAURUS
KAR-no-TORE-us

*T*yrannosaurus rex **was a famously ferocious predator.** Everything about it was scary ... everything, that is, except for its short, stubby arms! But even *T. rex* would have had better luck scratching an itch than *Carnotaurus*. This meat-eating dino lived about 70 million years ago, during the late Cretaceous period. Scientists think its puny forelimbs may have been so short that they were totally useless. But *Carnotaurus* made up for its tiny arms with its long, powerful hind legs. These may have helped this predator sprint at up to 35 miles an hour (56 km/h), about as fast as a galloping horse. *Carnotaurus* was distinctive among theropods (a group that includes meat-eating dinosaurs that walked on two legs) thanks to its bull-like horns. Experts think this hunter may have bashed its horns against its rivals' in fights over mates, like mountain goats do today.

DINO BITE

The name *Carnotaurus* means "meat-eating bull," referring to this dino's horns and its taste for flesh.

8

DINO BITE

Carnotaurus could barely move its tail from side to side, which would have made it hard for the dinosaur to turn while running.

DIGGING IT: SKIN IN THE GAME

Fossils are incredibly rare: It's possible that only about one bone in a billion becomes a fossil. It's far rarer for soft tissues such as skin and muscles to form fossils. So when scientists discovered a fossil *Carnotaurus* complete with its skin, they were thrilled. The discovery shows that this dino was covered with a random pattern of cone-shaped bumps surrounded by scales.

WINGED WONDER

YI   EE

It swooped through Jurassic skies on leathery wings, like a modern-day bat. But *Yi qi—Yi* for short—wasn't a bat at all. It was a dinosaur! Scientists long thought that there were only two types of prehistoric flying reptiles. One type were small, feathered dinosaurs that were the ancestors of birds. And then there were the pterosaurs, non-dinosaur reptiles that got airborne on a membrane of skin and muscle that stretched from an extra-long fourth finger. So when Chinese scientists started studying *Yi*'s fossil in 2013, they thought it looked strange indeed: This dinosaur had a bony rod sticking out from its wrist, a support for a membrane like a pterosaur's or bat's—but this leathery wing *also* sported a row of feathers along its front edge. Experts aren't yet sure whether *Yi* got around by gliding, like a flying squirrel, or if it was a true flier. Only one of *Yi*'s species has been discovered so far, so scientists hope future fossils will reveal more secrets.

COLORFUL CLUES

Yi's fossil contained tiny cells called **melanosomes,** which are responsible for producing color. Using a microscope, paleontologists were able to look at the structure of these cells to figure out what color they produced when *Yi* was alive. The answer? This bat-like dino was mostly black, with red or yellow spots on its wings and head.

DINO BITE

Yi qi is Mandarin for "strange wing."

DINO BITE

Yi was about the size of a pigeon.

11

PRE-REX

PROCERATOSAURUS   **pro-seh-RAT-oh-SORE-us**

The tyrannosaurs—*T. rex* and its toothy cousins—terrorized the late Cretaceous. They used a keen sense of smell to stalk prey, and enormous jaws bristling with knife-sharp teeth to rip it to shreds. The reign of these mighty reptiles lasted from about 99 million years ago until the dinosaur extinction 66 million years ago. But tyrannosaurs got their start long, long before that. An early tyrannosaur, *Proceratosaurus*, stalked what is now the United Kingdom during the mid-Jurassic, about 166 million years ago. *Proceratosaurus* was a smaller version of its fearsome descendants, probably measuring about 10 feet (3 m) from nose to tail. Like other tyrannosaurs, it had sharp, serrated teeth perfect for tearing flesh from bone. It also sported a showy crest on its nose.

DIGGING IT: FEISTY FOSSILS

The tyrannosaurs weren't just nasty to their prey—they were none too nice to their own kind either. Paleontologists have found gouges on the skulls of adult tyrannosaurs that suggest these animals bit at each other's faces. Were these battles squabbles over food, mates, or something else? Scientists aren't sure yet.

DINO BITE

Since its discovery in the early 1900s, scientists have argued about where *Proceratosaurus* fits in the tyrannosaur family tree.

DUCKBILL DINO

PARASAUROLOPHUS
PAR-ah-saw-RAH-loh-fuss

A FOSSILIZED PARASAUROLOPHUS SKULL

Seventy-five million **years ago,** a shallow sea stretched through the middle of North America. And herds of *Parasaurolophus* probably roamed its shores. It would have been quite a sight: Each of these dinosaurs was about as long as two cars parked front to back and as heavy as a full-grown white rhinoceros! *Parasaurolophus* was an herbivore that would have spent most of its time munching on plants. It could walk on two legs or switch to walking on all fours. Like other hadrosaurs, it had a wide, flattened, toothless snout a bit like a duck's beak, giving this group its name: the duckbills. Duckbills evolved in North America and eventually made their way to South America, Asia, and Europe. They even made it to Africa, a finding that shocked scientists, as that continent was completely surrounded by water at the time. This means that duckbills were probably powerful swimmers capable of paddling across water.

AWESOME ANATOMY: GET NOSY

Imagine if your nose stretched three feet (1 m) behind your head, then doubled back to connect above your eyes. That's what gave *Parasaurolophus* its incredibly odd face accessory. For a long time, scientists were stumped about the nose's strange shape. Now they know it was a kind of trumpet that allowed this dino to communicate with its herdmates over long distances.

KING OF THE DINOSAURS

A *T. REX* HUNTS ITS PREY, *ORNITHOMIMUS.*

TYRANNOSAURUS REX tye-RAN-oh-SORE-us REKS

It was a real-life monster. *Tyrannosaurus rex* hunted down its prey using an ultra-powerful sense of smell and ripped them apart with 60 banana-size teeth housed in jaws so strong they could crush a car. This bus-size superpredator ate anything and everything, from *Triceratops* to *Edmontosaurus*—and sometimes, even other *T. rex*. It had the strongest bite of any animal that ever lived on Earth— about 10 times stronger than a modern alligator's. And it didn't chew its food, but instead tore off huge pieces, threw its head back to toss them into the air, then swallowed them whole. *T. rex* probably had large home ranges, with no more than two individuals in an area the size of Washington, D.C. But these dinosaurs were such successful predators that over the 2.4 million years this species lived, scientists estimate about 2.5 billion of them roamed the Earth. That's a lot of teeth!

DIGGING IT: STRENGTH IN NUMBERS

The idea of one hungry *T. rex* is scary enough. Now imagine a whole pack of these predators chasing you down! Paleontologists long believed that *T. rex* was a solitary hunter. But when scientists discovered a group of similar tyrannosaurs that all died together, they theorized that these mighty hunters probably used teamwork to chase down prey—much like modern wolves do.

DINO BITE

A full-grown *T. rex* could have weighed nearly 20,000 pounds (9,000 kg)—making it about as heavy as an 18-wheeler.

DINO BITE

Scientists still debate why *T. rex* had such small arms.

THINK YOU'VE GOT WHAT IT TAKES TO ESCAPE A *T. REX*? FIND OUT ON THE NEXT PAGE.

FAQ COULD YOU HAVE OUTRUN A *T. REX*?

Imagine that you've time-traveled back to the Cretaceous. It's hot and humid, and sweat beads up on your forehead and drips into your eyes as you walk. You're making your way through a swampy forest when you hear a noise behind you. Oh no! It's your worst nightmare: a full-size *Tyrannosaurus rex*, and its eyes are locked on its prey—you. You have no choice but to take off running. If this scenario were possible, could you get away?

Many movies have depicted *T. rex* as a speedy and agile predator, capable of chasing down a human—or even a speeding jeep! But though this dino was fierce, it definitely wasn't fast, say scientists. In 2017, they developed a sophisticated computer model that estimated *T. rex*'s speed based on its body shape. The result? The king of the dinosaurs would have had a top speed of about 12 miles an hour (19 km/h). Most humans running for their lives probably could have evaded this predator. And the dino definitely wouldn't stand a chance against a car.

But even though you might have been able to outrun a *T. rex*, that doesn't mean you'd have been safe from one. There's strong evidence that these enormous killers hunted together in packs, like wolves. So you may have needed to outrun a whole pack to escape! Now that's a scary thought.

DINO BITE

T. rex had a brain twice as big as that of other giant carnivores of its time.

DINO BITE

Modern animals that hunt in packs include wolves, hyenas, lions—and even dolphins.

PUZZLING PLATES

STEGOSAURUS STEG-oh-SORE-us

This plant-eater was the size of a bus, with two rows of large, bony plates that ran along its back and a tail tipped with four wicked spikes. For a long time, *Stegosaurus* was a mystery to scientists. At first, paleontologists guessed that the plates may have covered the dinosaur's back like armor. It was only when they finally discovered a specimen that had been buried in mud—which held the plates in place as the dino fossilized—that they realized how the plates were really arranged. But scientists still aren't sure what *Stegosaurus*'s plates were used for. Did they help the animal stay cool or warm, or perhaps help it recognize its own species, or attract mates? There are also clues that suggest this dinosaur's spiked tail could have been a weapon: One *Allosaurus* tailbone sports a hole the exact size of a *Stegosaurus*'s tail spike.

A *STEGOSAURUS* SKELETON ON DISPLAY AT THE NATURAL HISTORY MUSEUM IN LONDON.

TAKING names

The Thagomizer

Dinosaur names usually come from the place where a fossil was discovered or the scientist who found it. But in the case of a *Stegosaurus*'s spiked tail tip—the "thagomizer"—the name comes from a cartoon! Gary Larson, creator of the "The Far Side" comic strip, called it that as a joke. Today, it's still sometimes used as the unofficial name for the body part!

DINO BITE

Stegosaurus means "roofed lizard."

DINO BITE

People once thought this dinosaur had a second brain in its rear.

21

MINI DINOS

NOT ALL DINOSAURS WERE BIG. MEET SOME TEENY-TINY MEMBERS OF THE MESOZOIC.

MICRORAPTOR

It was no bigger than a crow—but it was a ferocious predator all the same. *Microraptor*, a relative of *Velociraptor*, could fly or glide using its four feathered limbs. It spent most of its time zipping through the forest on the hunt for small lizards and mammals.

ACROTHOLUS AUDETI

This two-legged plant-eater stood no higher than an adult human's knee. It roamed the plains of what is now Alberta, Canada, about 85 million years ago. It sported a thick bony dome on its head, which it may have used to headbutt rivals.

PARVICURSOR REMOTUS

It may have been the tiniest dinosaur to have ever existed. A little smaller than a chicken, *Parvicursor remotus* had short forelimbs tipped in a single large claw, which it perhaps used to tear open termite mounds to get at the tasty insects inside. Its long, slender legs would have helped it speed away from bigger predators.

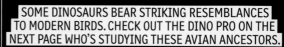

SOME DINOSAURS BEAR STRIKING RESEMBLANCES TO MODERN BIRDS. CHECK OUT THE DINO PRO ON THE NEXT PAGE WHO'S STUDYING THESE AVIAN ANCESTORS.

MAGYAROSAURUS

A creature the size of a horse might not seem little. But consider that other members of *Magyarosaurus*'s dinosaur family, the titanosaurs, were bigger than jumbo jets! *Magyarosaurus* was a titanosaur that got separated from its relatives on a small island, where it gradually evolved to be a smaller size.

23

Jingmai O'Connor, also known as the "punk rock paleontologist," is a curator of fossil reptiles at the Field Museum in Chicago, Illinois, U.S.A. She studies how, why, and when dinosaurs evolved into birds.

Because birds have such delicate bones, it is extremely rare for them to become fossils. So after earning her Ph.D. from the University of Southern California in 2009, O'Connor spent 11 years in Beijing, China. An area near Beijing is now farmland. But around 125 million years ago, it was covered in spewing volcanoes, lakes, and forests. When birds died, some would fall into the lake and their bodies would be covered by volcanic ash: the perfect recipe to make a fossil.

O'Connor helped identify the first fossilized lungs ever found from an early bird. She co-authored a paper describing a 99-million-year-old bird perfectly preserved in amber. She has also authored more than 100 scientific papers on ancient birds.

O'Connor has studied fossils all over the world, including in Mongolia, Romania, South Africa, Canada, and the United States. But she spends most of her time in front of the computer. While paleontologists do dig up fossils in the field, much of their work takes place in the laboratory, doing chemistry, or in the office, analyzing data. Paleontology comes in many forms!

"There's still so many crazy-cool things that are constantly being discovered. One discovery could change everything we think."

JINGMAI O'CONNOR

O'Connor in the field

CLAWED CREATURE

THERIZINOSAURUS   THERE-ih-ZIN-oh-SORE-us

This was one odd-looking dino, with a bulging pot-belly, a long, thin neck ... oh, and claws longer than baseball bats. *Therizinosaurus* dates back to about 70 million years ago, where it roamed what is now Asia. At about 33 feet (10 m) long and nearly seven tons (6 t), it was almost as big as a *Tyrannosaurus rex*. It was a close relative of velociraptors, but unlike its meat-eating cousins, *Therizinosaurus*'s small head and the shape of its teeth show that this dinosaur had adopted a vegetarian lifestyle. And despite its size and its enormous claws, experts think it was a slow and awkward mover, perhaps making *Therizinosaurus* easy prey for the many hungry hunters that roamed the planet at that time.

AWESOME ANATOMY: LOOKS CAN BE DECEIVING

Therizinosaurus's **three-foot (1-m)-long claws** were the longest of any animal's in the history of life on Earth. They may look like nasty weapons, but many scientists think the claws actually served a peaceful purpose: gathering leaves and branches and pulling them toward the dino's mouth.

DINO BITE

Therazinosaurus's long claws were once thought to belong to a giant turtle.

27

DINO HIGH
CLASS SUPERLATIVES

Biggest
Heavyweight

The record for largest dinosaur ever is constantly changing as scientists discover new species. But one of the top contenders for the title is surely *Argentinosaurus*. Paleontologists think it could grow to be more than 100 feet (30 m) long—that's the equivalent of three city buses parked end to end! And *Argentinosaurus* probably weighed in at about 90 tons (82 t)—as heavy as 13 African elephants! It may have been the largest land animal to ever live on Earth.

I've always looked up to you!

xoxo Anzu ♥

Brainiest, **pages 82–83**

Super Sprinter,
pages 140–141

Class Clown, **pages 152–153**

Most Likely to Succeed,
pages 208–209

GETTING A-HEAD

PACHYCEPHALOSAURUS   pack-ih-SEF-ah-low-SORE-us

Paleontologists once thought this dinosaur was a placid plant-muncher. Its flat, wide back teeth are characteristic of creatures that grind up plant material for their meals. But recently, paleontologists studied an unusually complete fossil skull of *Pachycephalosaurus* that included something never seen before: the creature's front jaw. To their surprise, the scientists discovered that while *Pachycephalosaurus* indeed had flat teeth in the back, it had serrated, knifelike teeth similar to a *T. rex*'s in the front. That's the same tooth system seen in modern omnivores—like humans— that don't just eat plants, but munch on meat, too. Next, scientists hope to find out what this dino was eating, by looking for tiny fossilized fragments of its past meals on its teeth, or by matching bite marks on fossils found nearby to *Pachycephalosaurus*'s mouth.

🔩 DIGGING IT: BATTLE SCARS

Why did *Pachycephalosaurus* have such an odd, dome-shaped head? Scientists have long debated whether this dinosaur used its 10-inch (25-cm)-thick skull for attracting mates, shoving rivals in the flanks, or butting heads with competitors. Then, in 2012, paleontologists found a *Pachycephalosaurus* skull that was dented in two places—evidence, they say, that it used its head in combat.

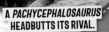

A PACHYCEPHALOSAURUS HEADBUTTS ITS RIVAL.

DINO BITE

Pachycephalosaurus's skull was more than 30 times thicker than the average modern human's.

ARMORED AND DANGEROUS

ZUUL   ZOOL

Even mighty *T. rex* would have thought twice before attacking *Zuul crurivastator.* This creature was an ankylosaur, a type of dino that scientists call a "living tank": Its low-slung body was heavily armored with rows of bony spikes. One specimen, found in Montana, U.S.A., was the most complete ankylosaur ever discovered in North America. It even included the dinosaur's long, club-tipped tail. Experts think ankylosaurs used their tails for self-defense, to whack at the legs of attackers. Some *T. rex* fossils have indeed been discovered with healed fractures in their lower legs, evidence that this theory could be true.

TAKING names
Celebrity Look–alike

In the 1984 movie *Ghostbusters,* Zuul was a demon that guarded the gateway to another dimension. When paleontologists first discovered the dinosaur species in 2016, they thought it looked just like the horned movie monster.

THE CHARACTER ZUUL IN THE MOVIE *GHOSTBUSTERS*

DINO BITE

Zuul's fossil was encased in a block of rock weighing 20 tons (18 t)—one so heavy that a forklift holding it sank into the parking lot.

DINO BITE

Some species of ankylosaur even had eyelids covered in armor!

DINO BITE

This dino's species name, *crurivastator*, is Latin for "destroyer of shins."

33

COLD WORLD

IT MAY BE HARD TO IMAGINE A DINOSAUR STOMP-
ING ACROSS A SNOWY LANDSCAPE. BUT NOW
SCIENTISTS KNOW DINOSAURS REALLY DID LIVE
IN POLAR REGIONS, WHERE THEY HAD TO CONTEND
WITH COLD WEATHER AND MONTHS OF DARKNESS.

PACHYRHINOSAURUS

Scientists have discovered hundreds of fossilized bones belonging to a small horned
dinosaur called *Pachyrhinosaurus* in the far
northern region of Alaska, U.S.A. These dinosaurs could have lived in the Arctic full-time,
or perhaps they only spent summers there and
migrated away when the weather turned cold.

FEATHERED MYSTERY

In 2019, paleontologists found 10 perfectly preserved fossil feathers in Australia dating back 130 million years, to a time when Australia was connected to Antarctica. It was the first evidence that feathered dinosaurs lived at the poles. Their plumage probably helped keep them warm—but no one yet knows which species the feathers might have belonged to.

LEAELLYNASAURA

Antarctic-dwelling *Leaellynasaura* may have traveled in flocks and fed on low-growing plants such as ferns. Scientists think that small herbivores like this one may have spent the coldest part of the year hiding underground. They have discovered burrows with dino fossils inside.

NANUQSAURUS HOGLUNDI

At 20 feet (7 m) long, this relative of the *T. rex* was about half its famous cousin's size. Scientists speculate that *Nanuqsaurus hoglundi* evolved to this smaller size to be able to survive the polar winters, when food would have been scarce.

A DINO NAMED SUE

Looking for the ultimate dinosaur experience? Make a beeline for Chicago, Illinois, U.S.A., to visit the famous Field Museum. It's one of the largest natural history museums in the world, with nearly 40 million artifacts, specimens, and fossils. And its crowning jewel is SUE, the most complete *T. rex* fossil ever found. SUE is also one of the largest *T. rex* ever found, standing 13 feet (4 m) tall at the hip and stretching more than 40 feet (12 m) long—almost half the length of a basketball court! And make sure to check out the museum's fossil of the titanosaur *Patagotitan mayorum* ... though since this critter is big enough to peek into the museum's second story, it's hard to miss!

1 Wear comfortable shoes. The museum spans nine acres (3.6 ha)!

2 Ever wondered what *T. rex* breath smelled like? You can find out at the Field Museum's dino exhibit!

TIPS FOR MUSEUMGOERS:

3 Seek out the Fossil Preparation Laboratory, where you can watch experts getting specimens ready for study.

4 Try out paleontology yourself: You can get hands-on with dinosaur bones at the museum's Crown Family Playlab.

37

TRIPLE THREAT

DINO BITE

More than 50 *Triceratops* skulls have been discovered in Hell Creek Formation, in Montana, U.S.A.

TRICERATOPS HORRIDUS   tri-SERR-uh-tops hoh-RID-us

It sported a massive frill, a strong beak-like mouth, and three sharp horns. *Triceratops* was one of the last dinosaurs to evolve on Earth before the planet was struck by the enormous asteroid that spelled death for most dinos. *Triceratops* lived all over western North America, surviving by nibbling on low-lying plants using its beak and the 800 small teeth that lined its jaws. Though it was a peaceful herbivore, it was one dinosaur that probably made predators think twice before attacking. Its skull alone could measure 10 feet (3 m) long, and it likely used its horns to defend itself: One *Triceratops* fossil has a missing horn, the spot scarred with bite marks that match the teeth of a *T. rex*. Paleontologists can tell that the bone healed after the attack, meaning the *Triceratops* survived the encounter to live another day.

AWESOME 🦖 ANATOMY: FASHION FORWARD

What was *Triceratops*'s frill for? It's been disputed by scientists for decades. Now most experts think that this unusual bit of anatomy helped *Triceratops* find mates. As these dinosaurs reached their teen years, their head frills ballooned in size. That suggests that frills were important only for adolescent and adult dinosaurs.

WANT TO LEARN MORE ABOUT DINO HEADWEAR? WE'VE GOT YOU COVERED ON THE NEXT PAGE.

FAQ WHY DID SOME DINOS HAVE HORNS?

Triceratops may be famous for its three horns, but it wasn't the only dinosaur to sport unusual headgear. *Styracosaurus* had a spike—tipped frill extending from the back of its skull. And *Kosmoceratops* had perhaps the oddest ornamentation of all: a downward—folding frill and 15 horns in all shapes and sizes.

You might assume that these dinosaurs used their horns to fight off pred-ators. But scientists say that likely wasn't the case. Many modern—day animals, from buffalo to Jackson's chameleons, have horns. And they don't use theirs for defense: Instead, their horns are weapons used to battle rivals of their own species in order to win mates. Like today's bighorn sheep, horned dinosaurs probably locked horns to fight each other. Scientists have even found wounds on fossilized *Triceratops* frills in the exact spot a rival's horns would have left a mark.

Some living animals, like certain species of African antelope, also use their horns to tell each other apart. Species such as waterbuck and kudu are closely related and their bodies look similar, but they have very different horns. Dinosaurs may have been the same way: Horns would have helped them keep track of who was who on the pre-historic landscape.

> **DINO BITE**
>
> Despite their fierce appearance, the ceratopsians, or horned dinosaurs, were peaceful plant-eaters.

> **DINO BITE**
>
> Only the inner parts of horns fossilize. In real life, dino horns would have been even bigger.

DINOSAUR GLADIATORS

IMAGINE IF DINOS FROM ALL ERAS AND AREAS COULD COME TOGETHER TO DUKE IT OUT. IN A MATCH OF HORNS TO TEETH, CLAWS TO TAIL SPIKES, WHICH PREHISTORIC BEASTS WOULD BE THE BADDEST BATTLERS OF ALL?

GLADIATOR NAME:
TALONS

SECRET IDENTITY: *Deinonychus*

ERA OF ORIGIN: Cretaceous

DEFENSE: five-inch (13-cm) claws on the second toe of each foot

CHECK OUT MY **PEDICURE!**

GLADIATOR NAME:
SPIKE

SECRET IDENTITY: *Gigant-spinosaurus sichuanensis*

ERA OF ORIGIN: Jurassic

DEFENSE: shoulder spikes

STEP CLOSER— **I DARE YOU.**

GLADIATOR NAME:
THE TANK

SECRET IDENTITY: *Ankylosaurus*

ERA OF ORIGIN: Cretaceous

WEAPON: a club-like tail

WHO WANTS A **"CLUB"** SANDWICH?

BIG AND BIRDLIKE

GIGANTORAPTOR jie-GAN-toe-RAP-tor

Picture something a bit like a modern-day ostrich. Now supersize it. That's *Gigantoraptor*, a Cretaceous-era critter that was more than 26 feet (8 m) long and 16 feet (5 m) tall—the height of a giraffe! In fact, it may have been even bigger: The single known specimen was not fully grown when it died. Most species shrank in size as they evolved into birds. Even *Gigantoraptor*'s direct ancestors were among the smallest dinosaurs. That made *Gigantoraptor*'s giant size shocking to scientists. It must have been a fearsome sight: When on the offensive, it spread out forelimbs ending in sharp claws, and it attacked prey with a strong, snapping beak.

S trange **Sc** ience:

BIG AND BIRDLIKE ... AND BALD?

Scientists think that oviraptors, the group that gave rise to *Gigantoraptor*, were covered with feathers. But *Gigantoraptor* itself probably wasn't. While most small dinosaurs and birds needed feathers to keep their little bodies warm, if *Gigantoraptor* was fully feathered, it would have overheated!

UNLIKE *GIGANTORAPTOR*, MOST OVIRAPTORS WERE PROBABLY FULLY FEATHERED.

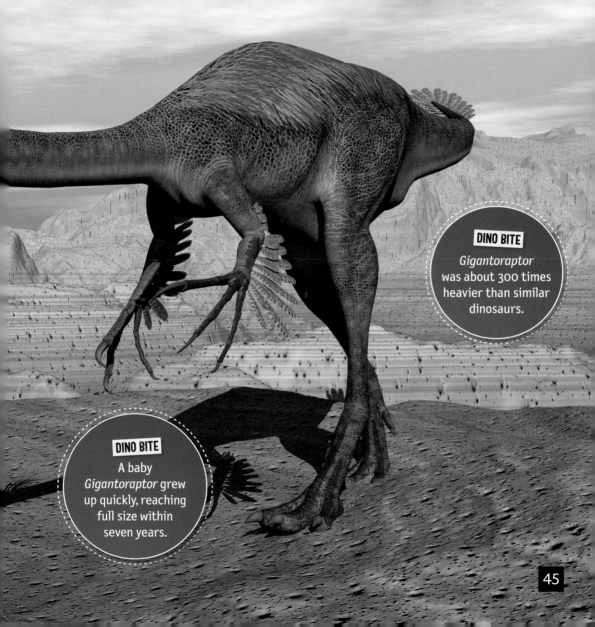

DINO BITE

Gigantoraptor was about 300 times heavier than similar dinosaurs.

DINO BITE

A baby *Gigantoraptor* grew up quickly, reaching full size within seven years.

BONE DRY

THESE DINOSAURS WERE DISCOVERED IN HOT, DRY DESERTS, PLACES WHERE FEW MODERN ANIMALS CAN SURVIVE. BUT BACK IN THE MESOZOIC, MUCH OF THESE LANDS WERE LUSH.

THE FIGHTING DINOSAURS

It's one of the most remarkable dino discoveries ever: a *Velociraptor* and a *Protoceratops* locked in deadly combat, discovered in the Gobi desert. Experts believe a sudden sand flow buried these dinos mid-fight, locking their bodies in place to slowly fossilize. At the moment of death, the *Velociraptor* had its deadly claw buried in the neck of its prey. The *Protoceratops* seems to have bitten and broken its attacker's right arm.

NIGERSAURUS

About 110 million years ago, in what is now the largest hot desert in the world—Niger's Sahara desert—lived *Nigersaurus*. It's nicknamed "the Mesozoic lawn mower" because it had more than 1,000 teeth! It wasn't small, at 30 feet (9 m) long, but experts think it still would have been prey for an enormous crocodile that shared its habitat.

TARBOSAURUS

While *T. rex* terrorized the landscape in North America, *Tarbosaurus* did the same in Asia. This carnivore, whose name means "alarming lizard" in Greek, had a large head and powerful jaws. It was at the top of its food chain, preying on other large dinosaurs in the floodplains where it lived.

LONG NECK

DIPLODOCUS ALSO HAD AN
IMPRESSIVELY LONG TAIL.

DIPLODOCUS   dih-PLOD-uh-kus

With its long, slender neck, *Diplodocus* could have dipped its head down low to sip up water, then swung it up high to nibble on leaves. Some scientists even think that, if a tasty crop of leaves was still out of reach, this massive dinosaur could rear back onto its hind legs, using its tail as a tripod to reach the tallest of treetops! It used teeth shaped like pencils to strip the leaves off plants. *Diplodocus* was one of the longest dinosaurs to ever live, with some species able to reach over 100 feet (30 m) from nose to tail. Its neck alone stretched about as long as a giraffe is tall. *Diplodocus*'s extremely long tail may have acted as a counterbalance for its neck. Some scientists think that this dinosaur could swing the tip of its tail so fast that it would create a sonic boom, like a whip cracking. Perhaps this was used to scare off attackers or communicate with others of its species.

ON THE MENU: EAT ROCKS

The plants that *Diplodocus* feasted on were tough and hard to digest. So this dinosaur would swallow stones that would grind against the food in its stomach to help break it down. This might sound strange—until you realize that many modern birds (living dinosaurs) do the same thing!

49

HORNED LIZARD

CERATOSAURUS seh-RAT-oh-SORE-us

This terror of the Jurassic had long fang-like teeth, a trio of horns on its face, and a row of bony spikes along its spine. It was a contemporary of *Allosaurus,* and, like that ferocious predator, *Ceratosaurus* probably gobbled up anything it could catch, from fish, turtles, and crocodiles to dinosaurs of all description. When it got prey within range, it would use its long, slender teeth to attack. These teeth—about four inches (9 cm) long—may have been so oversize that they stuck out when the dino's jaw was closed. Why *Ceratosaurus* would have sported such a toothy mouth is unknown to scientists. Experts also aren't sure what its back spikes were for or whether it could use its short arms for grasping prey. That's partly because fossils of this creature are incredibly rare.

AWESOME ANATOMY: RED-NOSED DINO

Scientists think *Ceratosaurus* may have used the bump on its nose to attract mates. During mating season, the bump may have turned bright red, like Rudolph the Red-Nosed Reindeer. Let's hope the other dinos didn't laugh and call it names.

SCIENTISTS THINK THAT *CERATOSAURUS* MAY HAVE HAD VIBRANT COLORS.

DINO BITE

This dinosaur was about 25 feet (8 m) long.

DINO BITE

Ceratosaurus's teeth probably gouged deep wounds in its prey.

FIERCE AND FEATHERED

DINEOBELLATOR
dih-NAY-oh-BELL-ah-tor

When paleontologists found a fossilized claw in a hillside in New Mexico, U.S.A., they knew it came from something interesting. Sure enough, it was the razor-sharp weapon of a new species of dinosaur called *Dineobellator notohesperus.* This dinosaur lived about 70 million years ago. It was a pint-size predator, standing only about three feet (1 m) tall at the hip and just about 6.6 feet (2 m) long. But it was a powerful hunter that probably used strong arms and hands to grab at smaller prey such as birds and lizards. It possibly used both its hands and feet to grapple with larger creatures. Its tail was stiff but flexible, making it an ideal rudder, like a cheetah's tail. That's evidence that this dinosaur would have chased down its meals with speed and agility.

AWESOME ANATOMY: BUMPY BONES

Bones from the forearms of *Dineobellator* have small bumps on the surface, places where feathers would have been anchored to the bone. Scientists think that all members of this predator's family were feathered.

DINO BITE

This dinosaur may have hunted in packs to take down large prey.

DINO BITE

The fossils of small dinosaurs like this one are rarer than those of larger dinos, because they are more likely to crumble away over time.

LAST MEAL

IMAGINE IF YOUR LAST MEAL WAS PRESERVED AS A FOSSIL FOR FUTURE SCIENTISTS TO INSPECT. THAT'S WHAT HAPPENED TO THESE DINOS. FOSSILIZED STOMACH CONTENTS CAN REVEAL WHAT AN ANIMAL'S LANDSCAPE WAS LIKE, WHAT CREATURES IT SHARED ITS HOMELAND WITH—AND EVEN WHAT TIME OF YEAR IT DIED.

SWALLOWED WHOLE

About 120 million years ago, a lizard named *Indrasaurus wangi* met an unfortunate end: It was swallowed headfirst by a feathered *Microraptor* (p. 22)! It's the fourth *Microraptor* scientists have discovered with preserved stomach contents. Together, the fossils show this creature snacked on whatever it could find: small mammals, fish, birds, and lizards.

PICKY EATER

This nodosaur is so perfectly preserved that paleontologists nicknamed its fossil the "sleeping dragon." Even this herbivore's stomach contents were intact, an especially lucky find since plant matter almost never fossilizes. The nodosaur's belly was full of one specific type of fern, meaning that this critter was particular about its food.

AQUATIC APPETITES

What does a 16-foot (5-m) sea monster eat for lunch? Paleontologists got the answer when they unearthed a fossil of a giant marine reptile called an ichthyosaur, preserved complete with its last meal in its belly. The beast was eating another kind of marine reptile: a thalattosaur, a creature that looked a bit like a human-size lizard.

SWIMMING SENSATION

SPINOSAURUS   SPINE-oh-SORE-us

Spinosaurus is most famous for the huge sail that ran along its spine. But until recently, this animal was only known from fossil fragments. Scientists had to make educated guesses about some parts of its anatomy, such as its tail. They thought it must have been long and narrow like those of its theropod cousins, including *T. rex*. So it was a surprise when, in 2020, they discovered a complete *Spinosaurus* tail—and found that it was actually huge, broad, and shaped like a paddle! It looked much like a modern crocodile's tail, showing that *Spinosaurus* may have spent much of its time underwater, hunting for fish. This was a shocking discovery for paleontologists: Decades of research has shown that dinosaurs of all shapes and sizes lived on land. Even *Spinosaurus*'s closest relatives walked on firm ground. The discovery of *Spinosaurus*'s unusual tail could mean that it was the first known species of dinosaur to have spent much of its time in the water.

SCIENTISTS NOW KNOW THAT *SPINOSAURUS* HAD A TAIL SHAPED LIKE A PADDLE.

The first ever *Spinosaurus* fossils, discovered in the early 1900s, were destroyed by British bombing during World War II. Drawings, photos, and descriptions were all scientists had to go on until 2008, when paleontologists were alerted that Moroccan miners had dug up a new fossil.

INFO ABOUT *SPINOSAURUS* WAS LOST TO HISTORY FOR DECADES, UNTIL ONE PALEONTOLOGIST MADE A BIG DISCOVERY. CHECK IT OUT ON THE NEXT PAGE.

57

DINO PRO:
NIZAR IBRAHIM

In 2008, paleontologist and National Geographic Explorer Nizar Ibrahim bought a cardboard box full of fossils from a man in Morocco. He'd found the box interesting and thought that possibly the fossils had all come from one dinosaur. But, other than that, Ibrahim didn't think much of the box, and he set it aside for a while.

One day, a year later, Ibrahim was looking at fossils with a group of other paleontologists in an Italian museum. They suspected the fossils were from a *Spinosaurus*, a dino that had been lost to science since the only known skeleton of it had been destroyed by a bomb in World War II. Looking at the fossils with his colleagues, Ibrahim realized something: These fossils looked a lot like the fossils in his box!

Sure enough, the bones in his box were all from the same dinosaur. And sure enough, that dinosaur was a *Spinosaurus*. Through these fossils, Ibrahim and his team discovered not only that the dino was a water-dwelling creature but also that it was an incredibly huge predator—perhaps the largest carnivorous dinosaur to ever live.

Ibrahim has made hunting for fossils in the enormous, scorching deserts of northern Africa his life's work. During the Cretaceous period, the area was covered in a network of rivers and teemed with life. Besides *Spinosaurus* and other dinosaurs, it was crawling with everything from 40-foot (12-m) crocodiles to huge pterosaurs winging overhead.

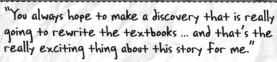

"You always hope to make a discovery that is really going to rewrite the textbooks ... and that's the really exciting thing about this story for me."

NIZAR IBRAHIM

Ibrahim among fossils found in the Sahara desert

TOOTHY TITAN

MAJUNGASAURUS **mah-JOONG-a-SAWR-us**

As human kids get older, their teeth grow loose, fall out, and are slowly replaced by a bigger set of chompers. That's nothing compared to what the dinosaurs went through: These animals lost many teeth over a lifetime, sometimes going through hundreds of sets! Paleontologists have found only a few complete skeletons of a meat-eating Cretaceous dinosaur called *Majungasaurus* ... but they've discovered hundreds of thousands of the dinosaur's teeth! That extreme number led experts to look inside the dinosaur's jawbones with special x-ray scanning. They found multiple teeth waiting to emerge, nestled on top of each other almost like a stack of ice-cream cones. That's similar to the anatomy of modern-day crocodiles and sharks, animals that continually replace their teeth throughout their lifetimes. Experts think that *Majungasaurus* would have gotten a new tooth in each socket about once every two months.

MAJUNGASAURUS HUNTS A GIGANTIC PREHISTORIC CROC.

DINO BITE

Cannibalism is not rare in nature: All kinds of modern animals, from insects to lions, eat their own kind.

S trange **Sc** ience:

Sulfer 32.06

21 Scandium 44.955908

DINO EAT DINO

Majungasaurus **had no shortage of sharp teeth** ideal for tearing into prey. But what did it eat? Tooth marks from this species on fossilized bones show that it chomped on just about everything, even enormous titanosaurs! It also dined on members of its own species, making it one of the few dinosaurs that scientists know for sure was a cannibal.

DINO BITE

This dinosaur roamed what is now the island nation of Madagascar, off the coast of Africa.

EGG-CITING FINDS

LIKE MOST REPTILES, DINOSAURS LAID EGGS.
BUT FOSSILIZED EGGS ARE RARE DISCOVERIES
THAT OFFER SCIENTISTS A PEEK INTO HOW THESE
PREHISTORIC ANIMALS BIRTHED AND RAISED
THEIR YOUNG. RARER STILL ARE FOSSILIZED EMBRYOS:
UNHATCHED BABY DINOSAURS.

BABY DINO

The baby inside an eggshell discovered in southern China was fully formed, curled up with its head tucked between its toes. It looked ready to hatch—but this baby was 66 million years old. Paleontologists say the fossil, nicknamed Baby Yingliang, was in a position just like that of modern baby birds inside their shells.

SLOW TO GROW

All teeth, from dinosaur chompers to human pearly whites, have lines that show their growth, similar to the rings of a tree. The lines on the teeth of a fossilized *Hypacrosaurus* embryo show it had spent six months inside its shell before it died. That surprised experts, because modern birds spend just weeks or a few months at most inside the shell. Scientists believe this extended shell stay would have made unhatched dinosaurs vulnerable to predators.

NICE NEST

In 2021, paleontologists in the Jiangxi Province of China found an oviraptor fossil sitting on top of eggs containing bones from embryos. These baby dinos were ready to hatch, proof that oviraptors must have been caring parents that tended their nests for a long time.

DOUBLE DIGITS

OKSOKO oak-soak-oh

The oviraptors were one of the most successful dinosaur groups of the late Cretaceous: Many of their fossils have been found in Asia and North America. And in 2020, researchers described a new discovery that might hint at how they adapted to their ecosystems. In Mongolia's Gobi desert, they found a group of four *Oksoko* oviraptors that had all been fossilized together. And unlike their three-fingered relatives, these oviraptors had just two fingers on each hand. The discovery shows that as they reproduced over many generations, these dinosaurs may have evolved particularly well to succeed in changing environments. Two fingers may have helped them eat a different type of food than their three-fingered relatives did—meaning they had less competition.

AWESOME ANATOMY: BIRD-BEAKED

***Oksoko* was an awesome eater in more ways than one:** It had a large beak similar to a modern-day parrot's. Like other oviraptors, it probably would have used this strong mouth to eat hard objects, such as tough fruits, shellfish, or eggs.

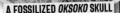
A FOSSILIZED *OKSOKO* SKULL

DINO BITE

This oviraptor was about the size of a large chicken.

DINO BITE

Young oviraptors roamed together in groups.

65

RUTHLESS REACH

MEGARAPTOR   MEH-guh-rap-tor

This was one truly terrifying predator. Twice the size of a modern-day giraffe, *Megaraptor* had a lean frame and long legs that made it more agile than *T. rex*. And where *T. rex* used its crushing jaws to rip apart its prey, *Megaraptor*'s weapons of choice were the long, sickle-like claws that tipped the ends of its muscular arms. Paleontologists think that it probably used its speed to hunt ornithopods, herbivores that darted about on two legs. Some experts think it's possible that this predator also snacked on baby titanosaurs. *Megaraptor*'s fossils date back to 90 million years ago, meaning that it was alive just before the dinosaur extinction. It was part of the theropod family, closely related to another of the Mesozoic's deadliest predators: *Allosaurus* (p. 92).

AWESOME ANATOMY: THUMB'S UP

When scientists found the first *Megaraptor* fossil in Argentina in the late 1990s, they thought the new dino was a larger relative of *Velociraptor*, with a long, slashing claw on each foot. Now they know that the claw they found actually came from *Megaraptor*'s thumb.

DINO BITE

This dinosaur was about as long as a city bus.

DINO BITE

Megaraptor's claw was about 14 inches (36 cm) long.

WHY WERE DINOSAURS SO BIG?

Dinosaurs were the largest land animals to ever live. Some titanosaurs were unbelievably huge: as long as three city buses parked end to end and heavier than 10 full-grown African elephants. In fact, the only animals in Earth's entire history that have grown bigger than the biggest dinosaurs are some whales—like blue whales. And their bulk is only possible because it's supported by water.

That makes dinosaurs' huge size a bit of a scientific mystery, and experts have debated several different possible explanations for the phenomenon. These explanations have included Earth's hot climate during the time of the dinosaurs, and the idea that being big helped herbivores fend off predators.

But, likely, we can thank dinosaur diets and their anatomy for their supersize statures. Being extremely tall helped sauropods reach high into trees where they could get food that other animals couldn't. (Think of modern-day giraffes but much, much bigger!) These sauropods had air sacs that extended from their lungs into their bones, making them much lighter than other animals would have been at the same size, and keeping them from collapsing under all that heft.

DINO BITE

Most carnivores alive today are about one-tenth as big as the predatory dinosaurs.

BABY DRAGON

BEIBEILONG **BAY-bay-long**

The ostrich is the giant of the modern bird world. But it's tiny compared to the ostrichlike dinosaur *Beibeilong sinensis*. This dino was likely around 20 times as heavy as an ostrich and laid two-foot (0.6-m)-long eggs in a nest the size of a monster truck tire! Eggs similar to the enormous eggs of *Beibeilong* have been discovered all over Asia and North America, but for a long time scientists didn't know what kind of dinosaur they belonged to. Then scientists found a tiny baby dinosaur curled up in one of the eggs. Its name translates to "baby dragon from China" for its huge feathered wings and dragon-like head. *Beibeilong* is a cousin of the oviraptors, such as *Oksoko* (p. 64). But while most oviraptors were similar in size to modern birds, this species towered over them all.

BEIBEILONG JUVENILES HATCH FROM EGGS.

DIGGING IT: MEGA-MOM

Like modern birds, oviraptors sat on their eggs to protect them and keep them warm. Their relative *Beibeilong* probably incubated its eggs, too. Few predators would likely have been brave enough to try to steal a baby from a three-ton (2.7-t) mama *Beibeilong*!

DINO BITE

Beibeilong laid about a dozen eggs at a time.

DINO BITE

One scientist described this dino as looking a lot like Big Bird from *Sesame Street*.

71

TRAPPED IN AMBER

SOME OF THE MOST INCREDIBLE FOSSIL FINDS EVER ARE ENCASED IN AMBER, THE FOSSILIZED RESIN FROM TREES.

MAMA BUG

This find is no dino, but this insect did live during the age of dinosaurs, in the early Cretaceous. The bug, called a scale insect, has 60 eggs attached to her body, and a few of her newly hatched babies can be seen in the amber around her. Scientists say it's the first evidence of 100-million-year-old insect parenting.

FLUFFY FEATHERS

On the rare occasion that preserved dinosaur feathers have been discovered, they are almost always pressed flat into rock. But amber kept these 80-million-year-old feathers in their three-dimensional shape. Even their gray, white, red, and brown colors can be seen. Scientists believe feathers like these are among the earliest that ever evolved.

RARE FIND

Owing to their small size, insects are the critters most likely to be encased in amber. That makes the discovery of an amber-covered miniature reptile in Myanmar even more special. It was about the size of a bee hummingbird, the world's smallest living bird. While scientists originally identified the creature as a tiny dinosaur, paleontologists now think that it may be a type of prehistoric lizard.

FABULOUS FEATHERS

EPIDEXIPTERYX EP-ee-dex-ip-ter-ex

If you saw *Epidexipteryx* from afar today, you might think it was just an ordinary bird. It was the size of a pigeon, with a feather-covered body and a plume of long tail feathers. But one glance at this dinosaur's claw-tipped arms and snapping teeth, and you'd know it was no regular bird! Scientists discovered an *Epidexipteryx* fossil preserved on a slab of rock. Impressions on its body showed the researchers where feathers had once been. But *Epidexipteryx* short arm feathers couldn't have given it lift. And its extravagant tail feathers wouldn't have been useful for flight either. Instead, paleontologists think this dinosaur probably used its tail feathers to woo mates, like a peacock does today.

A MODEL *EPIDEXIPTERYX* SKELETON

AWESOME ANATOMY: COMMON BONES

Epidexipteryx **did not fly.** But it had many features that link it closely to birds, such as a humerus, or upper arm bone, that was as long as its femur, or thigh bone. Scientific analysis reveals that this dinosaur was one of the closest relatives of flying birds.

74

DINO BITE

Scientists think dinosaurs first evolved feathers to keep themselves warm. Flight came later.

DINO BITE

Epidexipteryx may have had a skin wing, similar to that of a modern bat!

75

CHAMPIONS OF CHOMP

WHICH DINO SPECIES WOULD WIN IN A FOOD-EATING CONTEST? HERE ARE SOME OF THE MESOZOIC'S BIGGEST EATERS.

CONTESTANT 1

THE LAWN MOWER

SPECIES: *Sarmientosaurus*

WHAT'S FOR LUNCH?: low-lying plants

HOW HUNGRY?: This dino would sweep its huge head across the ground, gobbling up plants so fast it didn't stop to chew.

SCARFS ITS FOOD WHOLE!

CONTESTANT

2

PACK HUNTER

SPECIES: *Mapusaurus roseae*

WHAT'S FOR LUNCH?: massive herbivores

HOW HUNGRY?: These big carnivores may have worked together in packs to take down dinos 10 times their weight.

CONTESTANT

3

ONE HANGRY HUNTER!

TEENAGE *T. REX*

SPECIES: *Tyrannosaurus rex*

WHAT'S FOR LUNCH?: mostly herbivores such as *Edmontosaurus* and *Triceratops*

HOW HUNGRY?: In their teen years, *T. rex* ate enough to pack on nearly five pounds (2.3 kg) per day.

NOT A DINOSAUR

WHEN IT COMES TO PREHISTORIC ANIMALS, DINOSAURS GET ALL THE HYPE. BUT NOT EVERY TOOTHY PREHISTORIC CREATURE WAS A DINO.

DICYNODONT

This sheep-size creature had a beak like a tortoise's and front legs that sprawled out sideways like a lizard's. Dicynodont belonged to the therapsids, a group of prehistoric reptiles that became the ancestors and distant relatives of mammals. Despite their ferocious appearance, these were herbivores that used their unusual jaws to grind up vegetation.

MEGALANIA

It was the largest land lizard that ever lived, growing up to 16 feet (5 m) from head to tail. It was a predator that fed on large mammals, snakes, birds, and other reptiles (basically, whatever it could find). If you think it looks a bit like a modern Komodo dragon, you're right: These two carnivores are related.

DIMETRODON

It had a sail like a *Spinosaurus* (p. 56), but this was no dinosaur. *Dimetrodon* belonged to the synapsids, a group that was around long before the dinosaurs and eventually gave rise to mammals. (That means it was one of your great-great-great-great ancestors!)

AWESOME ARMOR

EUOPLOCEPHALUS YOU-oh-plo-SEFF-ah-luss

When it comes to armored dinosaurs, *Euoplocephalus* had especially spectacular armor. This dino was the Cretaceous version of a military tank, the size of a small elephant with back, head, and sides completely covered with tough bands. Each band was made up of a thick oval plate studded with short spikes. To have a chance of making one of these dinos a snack, an attacker would have had to flip it over to get to the only soft part of its anatomy: its belly. And that would have been no small feat: *Euoplocephalus* wielded a mighty weapon in the form of a huge club on the end of its tail. This dino took self-defense seriously!

DINO BITE

Armadillos have similar armor to *Euoplocephalus.*

AWESOME ANATOMY: ARMORED EYELIDS

Every bit of this dinosaur was armored—including its eyelids! *Euoplocephalus* had bony plates that it could flip up and down like shutters to protect its eyes. More than 40 nearly intact *Euoplocephalus* fossils have been discovered in western North America.

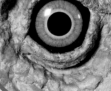

EUOPLOCEPHALUS'S ARMORED EYE

DINO HIGH
CLASS SUPERLATIVES

  **Brainiest**

It's tough to judge the smarts of something long extinct. But scientists can get an idea by looking at an animal's brain size compared to its body size. Humans have some of the biggest brains for our bodies in modern times, along with dolphins and chimpanzees. By that measure, *Troodon* was one of the smartest dinosaurs around. It used its intelligence for all kinds of complex behaviors, such as taking care of its nest and hunting small lizards and mammals. Still, experts think it was only about as smart as a modern ostrich. Hey, who are you calling birdbrain?

Let's be study buddies
next year!

♥ Deinocheirus

Biggest Heavyweight, **pages 28–29**

Super Sprinter, **pages 140–141**

Class Clown, **pages 152–153**

Most Likely to Succeed, **pages 208–209**

DIGGING DINO

ORYCTODROMEUS **oh-RIK-toe-DRO-mee-us**

A new dinosaur fossil discovery is always exciting. But when paleontologists found the remains of an adult and two juveniles in southwestern Montana, U.S.A., it was *where* the fossils were that gave the scientists a thrill: in a burrow! It was the first ever evidence that some dinosaurs dug shelters for themselves. The species, named *Oryctodromeus cubicularis,* was a small plant-eater that lived during the Cretaceous. It had powerful shoulders that would have helped it dig and a broad snout that it probably used as a shovel. The fossils probably belonged to a parent and its young, evidence that this dino cared for its little ones. Experts think the dino family probably built its home near a river, where they were buried by a sudden flood.

DIGGING IT: UNDERGROUND WORLD

As they investigated the dinos' burrow, scientists found multiple other smaller burrows connected to the main one. They believe these were the homes of burrowing insects. Today, burrowing creatures such as rodents often make their homes near burrowing bees, wasps, and beetles.

DINO BITE

Burrowing may have helped some dinosaurs survive in extremely hot or cold environments.

DINO BITE

Oryctodromeus may have nested in colonies.

WHERE SHOULD YOU

HUNT FOR FOSSILS?

DINOSAURS LIVED ON EVERY CONTINENT. IF YOU COULD JOIN A FOSSIL-HUNTING EXPEDITION, WHERE WOULD YOU GO?

START HERE

WHAT DO YOU WANT TO DIG FOR?

I want to see some famous fossils.

DO YOU MIND EXTREME WEATHER?

I can take the heat!

Let's keep things temperate.

I'll pack a parka.

Show me fossils from time periods that changed everything.

DO YOU PREFER THE DAWN OF DINOSAURS OR THE END OF THE ERA?

I want to know what happened when the dinos died.

Show me Earth's first dinosaurs.

CANDELEROS FORMATION

Temperatures in Patagonia, home of this formation, can hover around freezing for much of the winter. But travelers to this region will be rewarded with fossils of the titanosaurs, the most enormous animals that ever lived on land.

SAHARA DESERT

This African desert is one of the hottest regions in the world. But your sweat will be worth it when you take in fossils of some of the largest predatory prehistoric creatures ever.

HELL CREEK FORMATION

Make your way to Montana, U.S.A. Here you'll find fossils from an entire ecosystem as it was just before the asteroid struck.

ISCHIGUALASTO FORMATION

At this site in Argentina you'll find some of the earliest dino species, such as *Herrerasaurus* (p. 126).

87

NIGHT VISION

SHUVUUIA shu-VOO-ee-ah

Owls rule the night skies of Earth today, using exceptional vision and hearing to hunt in the darkness. Birds are modern-day dinosaurs, which made scientists wonder: Did any dinos do the same? Scientists analyzed the skulls of living nocturnal birds and extinct dinosaurs to see if there were similarities. They found that *Shuvuuia*, a pint-size predator dino that lived in what is now Mongolia, had vision and hearing similar to that of a barn owl. That means it could probably hunt in total darkness. Experts think *Shuvuuia* might have scampered around its desert home under the cover of darkness, using its keen senses to hunt for small animals such as lizards and insects. It used its long legs to outrun prey and its claw-tipped arms to dig burrowing critters out of their holes.

BARN OWL

AWESOME ANATOMY: PREHISTORIC PEEPERS

To judge how keen *Shuvuuia*'s vision was, scientists looked at a ring of bones that surrounded its pupil, called the scleral ring. The bones work like a camera lens: The wider they open, the more light can get in. *Shuvuuia*'s large scleral ring showed it had excellent night vision—likely better than most modern birds'!

DINO BITE

Shuvuuia was about the size of a chicken.

DINO BITE

This dinosaur had legs similar to a roadrunner's.

DINOSAUR DISEASES

DINOSAURS MAY HAVE BEEN MIGHTY, BUT THEY WEREN'T INVINCIBLE. JUST LIKE US, THEY COULD GET SICK AND INJURED.

TREMENDOUS TOOTHACHE

SUE the *T. rex,* a fossil on display at Chicago's Field Museum (p. 36), is famous for being one of the biggest of her species ever discovered. But even SUE suffered health problems: Its lower jaw is dotted with holes, the result of a parasite that infects some modern birds today. This infection, called trichomonosis, eats away at the jaw bones, causing extreme pain that prevents its victims from eating.

TENDER TOES

Dinosaurs suffered from some of the same diseases that afflict humans, including cancers. One hadrosaur called *Bonapartesaurus* had a growth on its foot that resembled a cancerous cauliflower. The fossil showed no signs that the cancer had spread, meaning the dino probably walked around with the tumor. This was one tough animal: Its fossil also showed two broken bones in its tail!

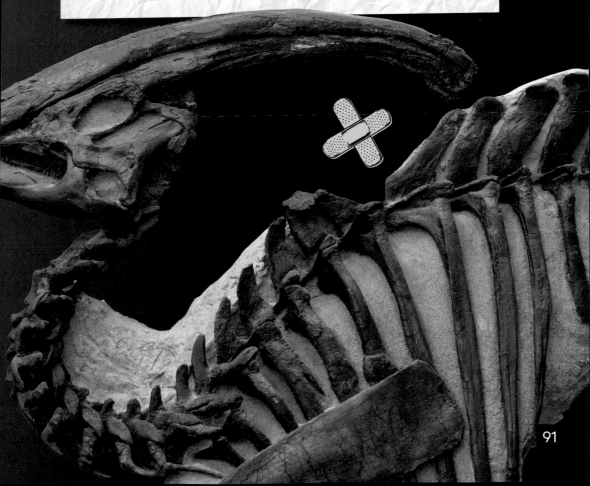

A PAIN IN THE NECK

One *Parasaurolophus* (p. 14) fossil, unearthed in 1921, was on display for decades when scientists noticed that something was wrong with it: The animal had a V-shaped indentation in its spine, the result of a broken back. Scientists think the injury happened when a rock or tree fell on the dinosaur. Amazingly, it didn't die from the accident: Its bones show signs of healing.

MIGHTY HUNTER

ALLOSAURUS AL-oh-saw-russ

With its eight-inch (20-cm)-long claws, 70 sharp teeth, and incredible speed, *Allosaurus* was one of the deadliest dinosaurs that ever lived. It may have used its huge jaw like a hatchet, slamming its upper teeth into prey and then tearing out flesh. This hungry hunter could have rivaled *T. rex* in size, reaching about 40 feet (12 m) long. But since *Allosaurus* lived about 85 million years earlier, the two predators would never have met. However, *Allosaurus* definitely faced off with another mighty dino: *Stegosaurus*. Paleontologists have discovered an *Allosaurus* tailbone with punctures matching the shape of a *Stegosaurus*'s tail spike, and a *Stegosaurus* neck bone with a bite mark that matches the jaw of an *Allosaurus*. That's evidence that these mighty dinos battled.

TAKING names

Strange Shapes

The name *Allosaurus* comes from Greek words that mean "strange reptile." That's because when the first *Allosaurus* fossils were discovered in the 1870s, scientists noticed that the vertebrae, or spine bones, were different from those of any other dinosaur known at the time. Now experts know these bones' unusual shape makes them light yet strong.

DINO BITE

Allosaurus could probably run at speeds of up to 21 miles an hour (34 km/h).

LARGER-THAN-LIFE PREDATORS LIKE *ALLOSAURUS* AND *T. REX* SEEM LIKE STUFF OF THE SILVER SCREEN— AND THEY ARE! CHECK OUT THE DINO PRO ON THE NEXT PAGE, WHO USES HIS SMARTS TO MAKE YOUR FAVORITE DINO MOVIES MORE ACCURATE.

When movie directors want to know what a *Gigantosaurus* might have sounded like, or how *Pyroraptor* moved through its habitat, who do they call? For the makers of *Jurassic World: Dominion,* that person was paleontologist Steve Brusatte.

Brusatte works at the University of Edinburgh in Scotland, and he earned his Ph.D. at Columbia University in New York City. When he's not busy teaching or discovering new species—an average of one per year for the past 13 years!—he has made it his mission to clear up misconceptions about dinosaurs. Thanks to his help, *Jurassic World: Dominion* shows dinosaurs with feathers—a first for the film series. And it portrays some species never seen before by fans of the films, such as pot-bellied, long-clawed *Therizinosaurus* (p. 26) and the enormous *Dreadnoughtus.* Of course, the film doesn't get everything right: Despite the title *Jurassic World,* nearly all the species it features lived in the Cretaceous!

Brusatte remembers watching the original *Jurassic Park* movie in a theater at age nine. "I thought the special effects were the coolest thing I had ever seen," says Brusatte. To be the newest film's paleontology adviser: "It's surreal!" he says.

"There's no better way for scientists to communicate our research to a huge audience all around the world than with a blockbuster movie."
STEVE BRUSATTE

BIRD OF MANY FEATHERS

SINORNITHOSAURUS
SINE-or-nith-oh-SAWR-us

Some 120 million years ago, groups of *Sinornithosaurus* probably hunted together, attacking small reptiles and mammals by leaping into the air and slashing with their powerful toe talons. A perfectly preserved fossil *Sinornithosaurus* discovered in China shows that this birdlike dinosaur had different types of feathers on different parts of its body, from short fluff on its head to long tufts on its arms and tail. While *Sinornithosaurus* was not large in size—only about three feet (1 m) long—it was probably a ferocious hunter.

A *SINORNITHOSAURUS* FOSSIL AT THE GEOLOGICAL MUSEUM OF CHINA

DINO BITE

Sinornithosaurus is one of the earliest known feathered dinosaurs.

DINO DANDRUFF

***Sinornithosaurus* may have been a cutthroat predator.** But among scientists, it's also famous for being one of the few dinos known to have dandruff! Fossilized flakes were found on the bones of a *Sinornithosaurus* fossil, as well as on the fossils of a few other birdlike dinosaurs. Experts say this shows that the dinos shed their skin in flakes, like birds, instead of in large sheets, like lizards.

DINO BITE

In 2009, a group of scientists published a study suggesting that—because of its grooved teeth—*Sinornithosaurus* likely had a venomous bite. Ultimately, there wasn't enough hard evidence to back up the claim, leading other paleontologists to disagree.

MUD DRAGON

TONGTIANLONG   tong-tee-ahn-long

Imagine a feathered, non-flying dinosaur the size of a donkey. That was *Tongtianlong*, a species discovered in Ganzhou, China. The fossil was discovered in an unusual posture, with its limbs splayed and its head raised. Scientists think it probably became trapped in mud and died while trying to free itself—lending this species its name, which means "muddy dragon on the road to heaven." The dino had a short head, a sharp beak, and a decorative crest on its head that it probably used to attract mates. It lived during the very end of the Cretaceous, about 70 to 65 million years ago. The fossil gives paleontologists a rare look at what Earth was like right before the enormous asteroid brought the reign of the dinosaurs to an end.

ON THE MENU: TOUGH STUFF

Tongtianlong **was an oviraptor,** a group of feathered, flightless dinosaurs with parrotlike beaks. Though they are not direct ancestors of birds, the oviraptors are closely related to birds. Scientists think that like many modern birds, this dinosaur would have used its strong beak to crack open hard foods such as nuts, eggs, and shellfish, as well as to munch on insects and plants.

DINO BITE

This fossil was found by chance, when a construction crew was blasting away rock with dynamite to make room for a school building.

DINO BITE

This dinosaur is related to *Oksoko* (p. 64).

POOP SCOOP

WHAT CAN YOU LEARN FROM A PIECE OF PETRIFIED POO? IT MIGHT SOUND GROSS, BUT MUCH OF WHAT PALEONTOLOGISTS KNOW ABOUT WHAT DINOSAURS ATE COMES FROM STUDYING COPROLITES: YEP, THAT'S THE SCIENTIFIC NAME FOR FOSSILIZED FECES.

BONE-CRUSHING JAWS

Only one *T. rex* coprolite has been discovered: The poo was about 1.5 feet (45 cm) long and contained a lot of broken bits of bone. Only a few carnivores alive today, such as spotted hyenas, eat bone. This was some of the first evidence that *T. rex* jaws had that kind of power.

STRANGE SNACK

Plant-eating dinosaurs in the late Cretaceous had all kinds of leafy meals to choose from. So why does duck-billed dino poo show that these animals were eating not only plants but also small crustaceans and rotting wood? Experts think that female duckbills may have searched for this unusual food in preparation for laying, as the extra calcium and protein would have helped them produce strong eggs.

BUGGING OUT

When experts used powerful x-rays to look inside a Triassic-era coprolite, they weren't prepared for what they saw: a perfectly preserved beetle seeming to peer right back at them! The coprolite came from a 33-pound (15-kg) reptile called *Silesaurus opolensis*, which used its beak to peck insects off the ground. The beetle was a totally new species!

SEAFOOD

In Poland, coprolites were found surrounded by 150-million-year-old pterosaur footprints. These coprolites showed that some of these winged dinosaur cousins ate small marine insects and shellfish, similar to the diet of modern flamingos. Like flamingos, the pterosaurs may have been filter feeders that scooped up water and food in their beaks and then strained out the water through bony plates that lined their beaks.

BIGHORN BEAST

COAHUILACERATOPS koh-WHE-lah-SAR-a-tops

This was one dinosaur that predators would have thought twice about attacking. *Coahuilaceratops* had the largest horns of any dinosaur ever discovered: They could be four feet (1.2 m) long—as long as a seven-year-old kid is tall! At around 22 feet (7 m) long and weighing some five tons (4.5 t), it was about the size of a modern-day rhinoceros. Even though its huge horns—one above each eye—might have been intimidating, *Coahuilaceratops* probably didn't use them as weapons. Instead, the horns were likely for attracting mates and fighting off rivals.

🐚 DIGGING IT: A FOSSIL HOT SPOT

***Coahuilaceratops* was the first horned dinosaur** to be discovered in Mexico. Today, the area is a desert. But about 72 million years ago, it was a lush swamp similar to the modern-day Gulf Coast of the United States. So many dinosaur fossils have been discovered there that scientists think the area may have been frequently hammered by monster storms that caused mass dino deaths.

DINO BITE

The smallest horned dinosaur weighed about as much as a cocker spaniel.

103

ROCK OF AGES

A journey along the Jurassic Coast is a journey through time.
Stretching for almost 100 miles (160 km) along the shores of southern England, this geological marvel features exposed sea cliffs that show layer after layer of rock spanning millions of years. Fossils are abundant here, especially after a good storm; storms erode the cliffs and reveal the remains of the marine creatures—including clams, sea snails, nautiluses, and ammonites—that once lived in the area's prehistoric seas. The coast's central portion, where many fossils from the Jurassic period have been uncovered, is its most well-known. It was here that Mary Anning (1799–1847), one of history's most important paleontologists, collected and sold fossils to help support her family. Over the course of her life, she made many significant finds, including the first plesiosaur, the first complete skeleton of an ichthyosaur, one of the first recognized pterosaur fossils, and the fossil fish *Squaloraja*.

1 Check the tides before you set out to search for fossils. Low tide is always the best (and the safest!) time to look.

2 Winter, when the beaches have fewer visitors and weather-related erosion is greater, is the best season to try fossil hunting.

TIPS FOR FOSSIL HUNTERS:

MARY ANNING

3 Be patient and dress comfortably! Fossil hunting takes time.

4 If you'd rather search for fossils indoors, the area has a number of museums and visitor centers where you can get up close and personal with some amazing collections.

TOOTHY LIZARD

EDMONTOSAURUS ed-MON-toh-SORE-us

One of the largest duck-billed dinos ever, *Edmontosaurus* was more than 40 feet (12 m) long and weighed in at a whopping 4.5 tons (4 t). It walked on four legs through swamps of western North America during the late Cretaceous period—unfortunately for it, it lived at the same time as *T. rex*, which hunted hadrosaurs like *Edmontosaurus*. Paleontologists have found partly digested hadrosaur bones in a *T. rex*'s stomach contents, and they even discovered a *T. rex* tooth stuck in an *Edmontosaurus* tail vertebrae! Scientists have actually discovered two different species of *Edmontosaurus*, known as *Edmontosaurus regalis* and *Edmontosaurus annectens*. Though both were found in the same region, the two species lived about seven million years apart. Unlike most hadrosaurs, *Edmontosaurus* did not have a crest on its skull. But it did have hollow nostrils that may have been covered by skin. When filled with air, these balloon-like sacs could have been used to make loud bellowing sounds.

 **AWESOME ANATOMY: SUPER CHEWERS**

Edmontosaurus had a birdlike beak near the front of its skull, which it used to chop plants and grasses—kind of like clippers. But it also had hundreds of small teeth, set back from the front of its jaw, which it used to chew them. Amazingly, below these rows of teeth were … more teeth! Like other hadrosaurs, *Edmontosaurus* had replacement chompers underneath its visible ones.

DINO BITE

Fossils showing *Edmontosaurus* skin impressions have revealed that it had scaly skin with a pattern of large bumps on it.

DINO BITE

Edmontosaurus means "the lizard from Edmonton." Its first fossils were unearthed in 1917 at the Edmonton Formation in Alberta, Canada.

MESOZOIC MAMMALS

THESE MARVELOUS (NOW EXTINCT) MAMMALS SCURRIED, SWAM, AND GLIDED ALONGSIDE THE DINOSAURS.

CASTOROCAUDA LUTRASIMILIS

Excavated by scientists from the bottom of an ancient lake in Inner Mongolia, China, *Castorocauda lutrasimilis* had the wide, flat tail of a beaver and webbed feet well adapted for swimming. Dating back 164 million years, it is one of the earliest mammals known to have been semiaquatic (meaning it lived partly in the water). Weighing about the same as an adult guinea pig, it was one of the largest mammals known to have lived during the Jurassic.

REPENOMAMUS ROBUSTUS

***Repenomamus*, which lived 125 million years ago,** is the largest known mammal of the Cretaceous period. A specimen of this three-foot (0.9 m)-long, badger-size carnivore found in China in 2005 was discovered with the remains of a baby dinosaur in its stomach!

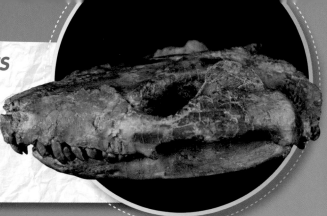

MAIOPATAGIUM FURCULIFERUM

One of the oldest known winged mammals, this furry Jurassic glider looked a bit like today's flying squirrels. *Maiopatagium*'s stretchy, parachute-like membranes allowed it to glide from tree to tree, feasting on vegetation.

FRUITAFOSSOR WINDSCHEFFELI

Insect-eating *Fruitafossor windscheffeli* was about the size of a chipmunk and ate the diet of an aardvark. It roamed North America 150 million years ago, using its strong claws to burrow for termites and to escape from predators.

FANCY FEATHERS

ANZU ANN-zoo

With its toothless beak, **towering crest,** and feathered arms and tail, 11-foot (3.3-m)-long *Anzu wyliei* looked a little bit like an enormous flightless bird. (Think of an emu or an ostrich.) But *Anzu*—which also sported a lizard-like tail and huge, sharp claws—was not a bird; it was a member of a group of two-legged feathered dinos called oviraptorosaurs. The bones of this oversize omnivore were unearthed in the fossil-rich lands of Hell Creek Formation, at sites in North and South Dakota, U.S.A. By studying rocks found with the bones, scientists determined that *Anzu*—one of the largest feathered dinos ever discovered in North America—inhabited a swampy, humid floodplain when it roamed the late Cretaceous, roughly 66 million years ago.

ON THE MENU: MODERN CLUES

How do scientists know what *Anzu* ate? They can tell by looking at its skeleton and comparing its physical features to those of animals that live today. The shape of *Anzu*'s jaw, for instance, suggests that it was able to slice off pieces of vegetation (plants). *Anzu*'s oversize curved claws are similar to those found on animals that snatch up their prey, indicating it may have eaten small animals. Prong-like bones found in *Anzu*'s skull are similar to those found in today's egg-eating snakes, suggesting *Anzu* may have also eaten eggs.

SPEAKING OF NAMES ... TURN THE PAGE TO
FIND OUT MORE ABOUT MESOZOIC MONIKERS!

 **FAQ** HOW DO DINOSAURS GET THEIR NAMES?

Why do we call *Anzu wyliei* "Anzu wyliei" instead of "Shuvuuia deserti"? Or "Epidexipteryx hui"? Or even ... "Fred"?

Scientists classify all living things as a way of organizing and understanding the millions of species that live (and have lived) on Earth. Classifying helps us understand how living things are (and have been) related to one another. In this system, organisms with similar traits are grouped together. The most specific groups they are sorted into are called "genus" and "species."

Scientists refer to animals by a two-word combination of their genus and species names. In *Anzu wyliei*, for example, *Anzu* is the genus name and *wyliei* is the species name. These "scientific names" usually come from Greek or Latin words, or they may be a "Latinized" version of a familiar word. By giving an animal a unique scientific name, scientists around the world are all using the same name for it, no matter which language they speak.

Like all living things classified by scientists, dinosaurs earn their names for a few different reasons. These can include their bodily traits or their behavior. Sometimes, the names of dinos are inspired by a person or by the place its fossils were found.

Anzu wyliei—whose name translates to "Wylie's feathered demon"—owes its genus name to a feathered half-lion, half-eagle creature from ancient mythology known as Anzu. Its species name, *wyliei*, was given in honor of Wylie J. Tuttle, the grandson of a longtime supporter of scientific research at the Carnegie Museum of Natural History in Pittsburgh, Pennsylvania, U.S.A., which houses the *Anzu* fossils in its collection.

TAKING names

What's in a Name?

Below are some common root words found in dinosaur names, along with their meanings. Can you spot any you recognize?

BRONTO = thunder	**RAPTOR** = robber
DINO = terrible	**SAUR, SAURUS** = lizard
MEGA = huge	**STEGO** = roof, cover
MICRO = small	**TYRANNO** = tyrant

113

TOP PREDATOR

THANATOTHERISTES tha-NAH-toe-THER-ist-ees

With a name like *Thanatotheristes*—Greek for "reaper of death"—it's no surprise this tyrannosaur was the top predator in its ecosystem. The 26-foot (8 m)-long meat-eater preyed on large herbivorous dinosaurs, including *Xenoceratops* and *Colepiocephale*, when it roamed North America approximately 80 million years ago. Though undeniably huge, *Thanatotheristes* wasn't as massive as its much larger cousin, *T. rex*, which reached lengths of 40 feet (12 m). *Thanatotheristes* is the oldest tyrannosaur ever found in Canada (and one of the oldest ever found in the world!), predating *T. rex* by about 13 million years. Discovering these earlier fossils offers scientists clues to understanding how the tyrannosaur family tree evolved over time.

AWESOME ANATOMY: COUNTING TEETH

From the 10 skull fragments found, scientists identified features of *Thanatotheristes*'s skull that they hadn't yet seen in other tyrannosaurs, including ridges along its upper jaw. *Thanatotheristes* had between 38 and 42 knifelike teeth in its upper jaw and at least 32 in its lower jaw—more than most other tyrannosaurs.

DINO BITE

Thanatotheristes had strong jaws that would have allowed it to keep a firm grip on its prey.

TURN THE PAGE TO MEET ONE OF THE PALEONTOLOGISTS WHO DISCOVERED THIS "REAPER OF DEATH."

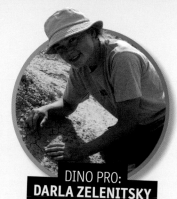

Thanatotheristes

was the first new species of tyrannosaur discovered in Canada in 50 years. And Darla Zelenitsky—assistant professor of dinosaur paleobiology at the University of Calgary in Alberta, Canada—was one of the researchers who added this "reaper of death" to the tyrannosaur family tree. She described the fantastic find in a 2020 paper, which she wrote along with several other scientists, including University of Calgary graduate student Jared Voris. It was Voris who had first recognized that the skull specimens looked different from any other species that had been seen before.

Paleobiologists study fossil animals and plants to learn more about the history of Earth—and the life that has evolved on it. Zelenitsky is particularly interested in the relationship between dinosaurs and birds. She was one of the researchers who described the very first dinosaurs in the Americas to be preserved with their feathers. She has studied the eggs, babies, and nests of dinosaurs, and she has worked with other scientists to describe not only new species of apex predators like *Thanatotheristes* and *Ulughbegsaurus* (whose fossils were unearthed from Uzbekistan) but also a turtle embryo-egg, the first ever reported soft-shelled dinosaur eggs, and a well-preserved oviraptorid theropod dinosaur embryo still in its egg.

> "Feathered dinosaurs have had a great impact on our understanding of early feathers and the link between dinosaurs and birds."
>
> **DARLA ZELENITSKY**

NO. 1 MOM

MAIASAURA MA-ya-SORE-a

Scientists named this duck-billed dino *Maiasaura,* meaning "good mother lizard," because the remains of adult specimens were discovered alongside many fossilized dinosaur nests. This discovery suggested that these late Cretaceous herbivores with crested heads were social animals that may have lived in nesting colonies, in which large groups lived together and raised their young. Along with broken dino eggs and hatchlings, scientists also found fossils of juvenile (young) *Maiasaura* specimens twice as old as those found at other dinosaurs' breeding sites. This tells scientists that *Maiasaura* may have actively looked after its young for an extended time, until they were able to go off on their own. It is possible that *Maiasaura,* which may have migrated in herds numbering in the thousands in search of food, took care of their offspring until they were independent enough to keep up with the traveling herd.

DIGGING IT: EGG MOUNTAIN

The site in western Montana, U.S.A., where *Maiasaura* was discovered earned the nickname "Egg Mountain," owing to the large number of eggs and nests uncovered there. Over time, hundreds of *Maiasaura* specimens have been found.

DINO BITE

Maiasaura used its toothless beak to snip plants and its hundreds of teeth to grind and chew them. Even on its herbivorous diet, it managed to top the scales at around three tons (2.7 t)— about the weight of the average pickup truck!

119

ANCIENT ANCESTORS

THOUGH THE MASS EXTINCTION EVENT THAT ENDED THE AGE OF DINOS WIPED OUT MOST SPECIES ON EARTH, MANY FAMILIES OF WATER-GOING CREATURES SURVIVED. CHECK OUT THESE ANCIENT ANCESTORS OF MODERN-DAY ANIMALS.

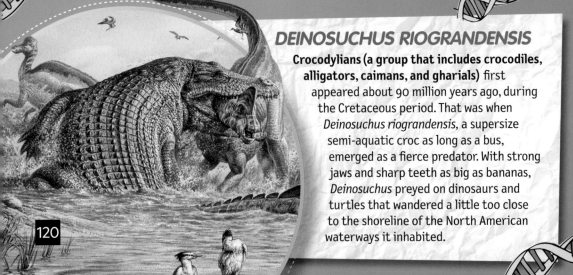

DEINOSUCHUS RIOGRANDENSIS

Crocodylians (a group that includes crocodiles, alligators, caimans, and gharials) first appeared about 90 million years ago, during the Cretaceous period. That was when *Deinosuchus riograndensis*, a supersize semi-aquatic croc as long as a bus, emerged as a fierce predator. With strong jaws and sharp teeth as big as bananas, *Deinosuchus* preyed on dinosaurs and turtles that wandered a little too close to the shoreline of the North American waterways it inhabited.

PORTUGALOPHIS LIGNITES

At one time, scientists thought the earliest snakes slithered about 100 million years ago. But in 2015, a study revealed that the fossilized remains of four ancient snake species found in Europe and the United States dated back tens of millions of years earlier than that. One of the finds was *Portugalophis lignites*, a snake that slithered around what is now Portugal eating small mammals, reptiles, and amphibians between 157 and 152 million years ago. Now that's s-s-s-super old!

ARCHELON

Archelon, **which swam in late Cretaceous waters munching on fish, squid, and plants,** looked similar to today's leatherback sea turtle. *Archelon* tipped the scales at more than two tons (1.8 t) and was from beak to tail about twice the length of an adult human.

SHARKS

These enduring apex predators have survived all five of Earth's mass extinction events. Fossil records show that sharks have been swimming in Earth's oceans for 450 million years—around 200 million years *before* the first dinosaurs! Scientists estimate that relatives of modern cow sharks (a member of the family Hexanchidae) had appeared by the Jurassic period.

SAIL AWAY

AMARGASAURUS ah-MAR-gah-SORE-us

To call *Amargasaurus* unusual seems like an understatement. Compared with other sauropods, it was kind of on the small side: only around 36 feet (11 m) long. And while most sauropods had super-long necks that allowed them to reach high into trees to feed, *Amargasaurus* had a relatively short neck that likely forced it to feast on vegetation much lower to the ground. But what really makes *Amargasaurus* a distinctive dino is the double row of spines spanning down its neck and back—the largest seen on any sauropod. The spines, which grew out of its backbone, restricted its movement vertically, which is another reason it had to stick to low-growing plants. *Amargasaurus* lived 130 million years ago, during the early Cretaceous period, in what is now Argentina.

AWESOME ANATOMY: MYSTERY SPINES

The details of the supersize structure rising from *Amargasaurus*'s neck and back are still a bit of a mystery. Some scientists think the spines were connected by skin, making them look like two giant, parallel sails. Others have suggested the spines were covered individually in keratin, the protein found in our hair and nails and in animal horns and hooves. And their purpose? Also a mystery. *Amargasaurus* may have rattled its spines to make some noise, used them for defensive purposes, or sported them simply for display.

DINO BITE

Like other sauropods, *Amargasaurus* could have used its tail as a whip to defend itself against predators.

DINO BITE

Based on the fossil evidence, scientists believe *Amargasaurus* didn't have very good hearing.

123

MOST MISUNDERSTOOD DINOS

I WAS **FALSELY** ACCUSED!

THESE CONTESTANTS ARE VYING FOR THE TITLE OF MOST MISUNDERSTOOD DINO. IMAGINE YOU'RE THE JUDGE OF THIS CURIOUS CONTEST. WHICH HAS THE STRONGEST CASE?

CONTESTANT **1**

OVIRAPTOR

"Because I was discovered near a nest of eggs that scientists believed belonged to the horned *Protoceratops*, I was given the name *Oviraptor*, meaning 'egg thief.' As if! I was no egg snatcher: Scientists later found an oviraptorid dinosaur inside one of these eggs, along with other oviraptorid skeletons sitting atop a nest of eggs. This made them realize I was actually incubating and protecting the eggs."

VELOCIRAPTOR

"The 'raptors' in the 1993 movie *Jurassic Park* more closely resembled my larger cousin *Deinonychus*. In the movie, the six-foot (1.8 m)-tall raptors are in hot pursuit of humans. In reality, I stood barely two feet (0.6 m) high, about the height of a medium-size dog. As in the movie, I did use my hooked, sharp claws to snare my prey, but that included small mammals and baby dinos—not people trying to clone my genetic material."

I WAS THE **VICTIM** OF **MISTAKEN IDENTITY!**

I DID NOT HAVE A **BUTT BRAIN!**

STEGOSAURUS

"At one time, scientists thought there might be a second brain in my rear that controlled my back legs and tail. After all, I did have a very small brain compared with the size of my very large body. Could that bump on my rump be a bonus brain that fed signals from the back of my body to the main brain, they wondered? Let me clear it up: No, I—I did not have a butt brain."

125

EARLY DINO

HERRERASAURUS huh-RARE-ah-SORE-us

*H*errerasaurus dates back about 230 million years, to the late Triassic period. That makes this two-legged carnivore one of the oldest known dinos—or dino cousins. For many years after the discovery of its incomplete skeleton, in the late 1950s, scientists debated whether *Herrerasaurus* was a "true" dinosaur or just an early close relative of dinosaurs. In 1988, the paleontologist Paul Sereno discovered a complete skull, along with more fossil fragments, in the Ischigualasto region of northwest Argentina. These new finds gave scientists enough information to reconstruct the ancient animal, which had powerful hind legs and short arms featuring three backward-curving claws that it could use for clutching and collecting prey. Many experts now believe that *Herrerasaurus* was an early theropod—and a real dinosaur after all.

S trange Sc ience:
THE LAND BEFORE DINOS

Though dinos would eventually evolve to become the dominant predators on land, early dinosaurs like *Herrerasaurus* were often smaller than other non-dino reptiles of their time. One of those hulking non-dino reptiles was *Postosuchus*, a distant cousin of modern crocodiles and an apex predator of the late Triassic. About 15 feet (4.6 m) long and eight feet (2.4 m) high, *Postosuchus* used its serrated teeth, sharp claws, and impressive heft to ambush its prey in forests of what is now the American Southwest.

DINO BITE

Herrerasaurus means "Herrera's lizard." It was named for Victorino Herrera, the rancher who discovered the first specimen.

TERRIFIC PTEROSAURS

PTEROSAURS WERE NOT DINOSAURS! THEY WERE WINGED REPTILES OF DIFFERENT SIZES THAT GLIDED THROUGH SKIES FROM THE LATE TRIASSIC TO THE END OF THE CRETACEOUS PERIOD.

PTERODACTYLUS

Like all pterosaurs, *Pterodactylus* had a wing membrane of skin and muscle that stretched from its long fourth finger to its legs. Fitting, then, that the name *Pterodactylus* comes from *pterodaktulos*, a Greek word that means "winged finger." *Pterodactylus* was the first pterosaur ever discovered. It was identified in 1784 by Cosimo Collini, an Italian scientist who actually thought the unusual creature used its wings to paddle through water!

PTERANODON

Pteranodon had toothless, pelican-like jaws that it used to scoop up fish from surface waters during the late Cretaceous. It had an impressive wingspan of about 23 feet (7 m)—about twice that of the wandering albatross, which has the largest known wingspan of any living bird.

QUETZALCOATLUS

Quetzalcoatlus was the largest flying animal ... ever. The late Cretaceous creature was as big as a giraffe and had a wingspan that rivaled that of a jet! To get itself off the ground, Quetzalcoatlus may have crouched and then hurled itself into the air before flapping its expansive wings to take off. Like today's birds, Quetzalcoatlus had hollow bones that helped it fly.

DIMORPHODON

Early Jurassic Dimorphodon was one of the earliest ptero-saurs. At only about three feet (1 m) long, it was about half the size of Pteranodon with a wingspan only one-quarter as wide. Dimorphodon used its sharp teeth to tear apart the fish it grabbed while skimming over the top of the water. It had a long tail with a diamond-shaped flap at the end that likely worked as a "rudder," helping to stabilize it as it flew.

TOTAL BONEHEAD

GASTONIA gas-TONE-ee-ah

Like other herbivores, *Gastonia* needed to get serious about defending itself if it was going to survive in a world populated by strong-jawed meat-eating predators. *Gastonia* was covered from head to tail with heavy armor, including rows of flat, sideways-pointing spikes on each side of its low-slung body and tail. Unlike other similarly well-armored ankylosaurs, its tail wasn't capped with a club. But its tail's bladelike protrusions could have been used to whack its aggressors, including *Utahraptor*, the apex predator of its habitat. *Gastonia* lived about 125 million years ago, during the early Cretaceous period, when it used its leaf-shaped teeth to dine on plants in the woodlands of western North America.

AWESOME ANATOMY: SHOCK-ABSORBING SKULL

***Gastonia* had a pretty tough noggin.** Its skull features suggest to scientists that the armored, plated dino may have engaged in some serious headbutting. Wide, domed, and extra-thick, its skull seemed designed to take a few hits: A joint around the bones that contained its brain may have provided some "shock absorption" for those times *Gastonia* was, well, using its head.

DINO BITE

Gastonia's brain was about the size of a chicken egg.

DINO BITE

Gastonia weighed about as much as the Liberty Bell.

131

START HERE.

WHICH
DINO PET
WOULD YOU GET?

OK, OK—OF COURSE YOU CAN'T ACTUALLY HAVE A DINOSAUR FOR A PET. BUT IF YOU COULD, WHICH ONE WOULD BE THE BEST MATCH FOR YOU?

HOW MUCH SPACE DO YOU HAVE?

It's kind of tight around here.

LOOKING FOR A FRIEND WITH FANTASTIC FEATHERS OR AWESOME ARMOR?

Feathers are first-class.

I'm all about armor.

Lots of room to move!

WANT TO DINE WITH A MEAT-EATER OR A PLANT-EATER?

Just greens, please.

EYE-CATCHING HEADGEAR OR A NECK LONG ENOUGH TO REACH THAT FRISBEE THAT KEEPS GETTING STUCK IN THE TREE?

Bring on the carnivores!

WANT TO RUN AROUND THE PARK OR GO FOR A SWIM WITH YOUR SIDEKICK?

Run!

Swim!

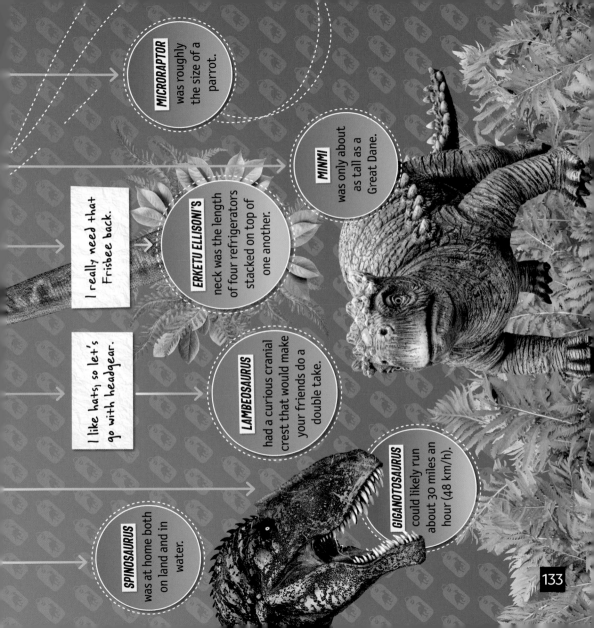

MICRORAPTOR was roughly the size of a parrot.

MINMI was only about as tall as a Great Dane.

ERKETU ELLISONI'S neck was the length of four refrigerators stacked on top of one another.

I really need that Frisbee back.

I like hats, so let's go with headgear.

LAMBEOSAURUS had a curious cranial crest that would make your friends do a double take.

GIGANOTOSAURUS could likely run about 30 miles an hour (48 km/h).

SPINOSAURUS was at home both on land and in water.

133

RUFFLING FEATHERS

KULINDADROMEUS   KOO-lin-dah-DRO-mee-us

One of the coolest things scientists have ever learned about dinosaurs is that they had feathers. Specifically, they found that meat-eating dinosaurs called theropods had them. These "raptors" are considered to be direct ancestors of modern-day birds, which also have feathers. But the discovery in Siberia of Jurassic dino *Kulindadromeus* revealed that it wasn't only theropods that had feathers: *Kulindadromeus* was an ornithischian (bird-hipped dinosaur), an herbivore that had both scales and feather-like structures on its 4.5-foot (1.5-m) body. The scientists who unearthed the fossils believe that this discovery means that feathers could have been more widespread than previously thought.

AWESOME ANATOMY: DINO HAIRDO

The *Kulindadromeus* fossils showed that the Jurassic period plant-eater actually had several different types of feathers. It sported short bristles on its head, neck, and body, something scientists call "dino fuzz." It also had feathery tufts on its upper arm and thigh, as well as ribbon-shaped feathers on its lower leg that scientists hadn't ever seen before.

DINO BITE

Dating back 160 million years, *Kulindadromeus* is the earliest dinosaur with feather-like structures that scientists have discovered so far.

DINO BITE

Feathers probably first evolved during the Triassic period—most likely for insulation.

135

UNDER THE SEA

WHILE DINOSAURS MAY HAVE DOMINATED THE LANDS OF THE MESOZOIC, A WHOLE HOST OF EQUALLY INTIMIDATING AQUATIC ANIMALS WERE MOVING THROUGH EARTH'S WATERS.

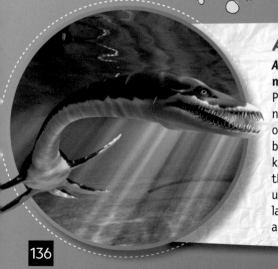

ALBERTONECTES

Albertonectes was part of a group of marine reptiles called plesiosaurs. Plesiosaurs had small heads but huuuge necks, and *Albertonectes* had the hugest one of all: 23 feet (7 m) long with 76 neck bones—more than any other animal known to date. Its neck was longer than the rest of its entire body! *Albertonectes* used its flippers and tail to move through late Cretaceous waters looking for squid and fish.

LIOPLEURODON

Jurassic predator *Liopleurodon* had pointed, sharp teeth inside some seriously powerful jaws. It was a pliosaur, a type of plesiosaur with shorter necks and bigger heads than relatives like *Albertonectes*. They did enjoy some of the same snacks, though: *Liopleurodon* also dined on fish and squid, though its massive jaws would have allowed it to take down even larger prey.

TYLOSAURUS

***Tylosaurus* was an ambush hunter** that used its powerful tail and flippers to reach a variety of prey, including sharks, turtles, and plesiosaurs. *Tylosaurus* was a mosasaur, a prehistoric reptile that is a relative of modern-day snakes and monitor lizards. It is the official state marine fossil of Kansas, U.S.A., which was once covered by a shallow sea inhabited by the late Cretaceous creature.

OPHTHALMOSAURUS

***Ophthalmosaurus* was an ichthyosaur,** a group of marine reptiles whose fossil remains show that they lived throughout almost the entire Mesozoic era. *Ophthalmosaurus* may have used its oversize peepers to hunt prey in the low-light conditions of deeper waters. Researchers believe it may have been able to dive to depths of 1,600 feet (500 m) or more.

THAT'S FISHY

LIAONINGOSAURUS   LEE-ow-ning-oh-SORE-us

Liaoningosaurus was a pretty unusual ankylosaur. It lived between 125 and 121 million years ago—much earlier than some of the better-known armored dinos, such as late Cretaceous *Ankylosaurus*. And it was much smaller: just over a foot (30 cm) long. *Liaoningosaurus* looked a bit like a turtle! But the most unusual thing about this pint-size plant-eater? It may not have been only a plant-eater. Ankylosaurs are known to be herbivores, but fossil remains of *Liaoningosaurus* that were unearthed in northeastern China suggested that it may have had a more diverse diet: Scientists found parts of fish skeletons inside *Liaoningosaurus*'s rib cage. This means it may have also eaten fish—making it perhaps the first carnivore in its family. The scientists that discovered *Liaoningosaurus* also found that its teeth were not triangular or leaf-shaped, as most ankylosaur teeth are. Instead, its teeth were shaped kind of like forks—perfect for snagging and eating fish!

 DIGGING IT: EXAMINING THE EVIDENCE

Scientists have offered some other explanations for why fish skeletons could have found their way inside *Liaoningosaurus*'s remains. Perhaps when *Liaoningosaurus* died, its body settled atop fish that were already dead. Or maybe the fish were taking cover inside the dino's remains when they also met their end. But the scientists who wrote about *Liaoningosaurus* think it was indeed a fish-eater.

DINO BITE

Liaoningosaurus was found in China's Yixian Formation, a geological formation where sauropods, tyrannosaurs, and ceratopsians (beaked dinos) have also been found.

DINO BITE

A piscivore is a carnivore that eats mostly fish.

139

DINO HIGH
CLASS SUPERLATIVES

Super Sprinter

Its name may mean "chicken mimic," but *Gallimimus* isn't afraid to leave every other dino in the dust. Built like an ostrich—the world's fastest bird—this 20-foot (6-m)-long late Cretaceous ornithomimid used its long legs to sprint at speeds of up to possibly 50 miles an hour (80 km/h), making it the fastest dino. It achieved this speed despite its considerable heft—it weighed half a ton (450 kg)! With its toothless, birdlike beak, *Gallimimus* feasted on seeds, leaves, insects, and probably small mammals.

Keep running like the wind!

Your pal, Troodon

Next year you'll make it
all the way to the state finals!

—Coach

Biggest Heavyweight,
pages 28–29

Brainiest, **pages 82–83**

Class Clown, **pages 152–153**

Most Likely to Succeed,
pages 208–209

APEX PREDATOR

GNATHOVORAX   NATH-oh-VOR-ax

Fossil evidence of predatory dinosaurs during the Triassic period isn't as plentiful as during the Jurassic and Cretaceous, so the well-preserved remains of early predator *Gnathovorax* are a pretty spectacular find. Researchers found its mostly complete skeleton lying on its right side in a layer of mudstone in southern Brazil in 2014. They dated the remains to 233 million years ago, when South America was still part of the supercontinent Pangaea. At "only" half a ton (450 kg) and 10 feet (3 m) long, *Gnathovorax* was the biggest predatory dinosaur of its time and place—and is the oldest meat-eating dinosaur found to date. *Gnathovorax* had long claws perfect for capturing prey and sharp, serrated teeth suited for tearing into flesh.

Strange **Sc**ience: HIGH-TECH PALEONTOLOGY

Gnathovorax **was in such good condition** when it was found that researchers were able to put its skull in a CT scanner and reconstruct its brain. (A CT scanner takes x-rays from different angles to create a 3D image of a creature's bones and soft tissues.) They determined that *Gnathovorax* likely had good coordination and eyesight, which would have helped it cement its status as apex predator.

DINO BITE

Gnathovorax roughly translates to "a jaw for devouring things."

DINO BITE

Gnathovorax was part of the family known as Herrerasauridae, which became extinct by the end of the Triassic period.

143

EXTINCT ODDITIES

THESE EXTRAORDINARY ANIMALS LIVED IN THE YEARS BEFORE THE DINOSAURS TOOK OVER THE PLANET.

TRILOBITES

Trilobites were abundant in Earth's waters from about 521 to 250 million years ago, and evidence of these creatures has been found all over the world. They are one of the earliest known arthropods, a group that today includes spiders, insects, and crustaceans. During their incredible 270-million-year run, trilobites evolved into more than 25,000 species of all shapes and sizes.

EURYPTERIDS

Like trilobites, eurypterids were long-lasting, water-going arthropods. Looking a bit like horseshoe crabs or scorpions, most were on the small side, but one species, *Jaekelopterus rhenaniae*, grew to be the largest arthropod ever: around eight feet (2.5 m) long! Eurypterids inhabited brackish (a mix of salty and fresh) waters from more than 400 million to about 251 million years ago.

GRIFFINFLIES

What a wingspan! Griffinflies are the largest known insects of all time: Their wingspan reached a whopping 27 inches (69 cm)—more than three times the wingspan of a modern-day dragonfly. Griffinflies flapped their phenomenally huge wings between 300 and 280 million years ago.

ARTHROPLEURA

Like bugs? There's plenty to love about *Arthropleura*—literally! At more than six feet (1.8 m) long and 1.5 feet (0.5 m) wide, this oversize invertebrate was the largest land-living "bug" to ever scurry around Earth. Looking a bit like a massive millipede, it inhabited swamps between 320 and 290 million years ago in what is now North America and Europe.

DINOSAUR RIDGE, COLORADO, U.S.A.

FOLLOWING FOOTSTEPS

Some pretty amazing dinosaur remains have been uncovered in the Morrison Fossil Area, west of Denver, Colorado. In 1877, a professor named Arthur Lakes discovered the world's first known *Apatosaurus* and *Stegosaurus* fossils there. And then, during the construction of a roadway in 1937, workers came across hundreds of dino tracks left by duck-billed herbivores and theropods. Even today, fossils and tracks can be found in the layers of rock that make up this region, known as Dinosaur Ridge. During the Jurassic and Cretaceous periods, the area was first covered by slow-moving rivers and then an inland sea. Dinosaurs lived by the rivers and the western edge of this inland sea; some that died were buried under sand and mud. The draining of the sea was followed by uplift of the earth that created mountains, which was then followed by a period of intense erosion that revealed the seabed layers.

1 Stop by the Main Visitor Center to view a variety of fossils and bones, including a *Triceratops* skull, *T. rex* teeth, and *Iguanodon* thumb spikes.

2 No water is available along the trail, so bring your own!

3 Don't forget to wear sunscreen and comfy shoes. Bring layers to be prepared for weather changes.

4 Tour Dinosaur Ridge Trail, home to more than 300 dinosaur tracks. You can take a guided bus tour or a guided walking tour.

Cretaceous Comics presents...

NAME ACCLAIM!

IMAGINE YOU ARE CASTING THE NEXT BIG SUPERHERO MOVIE. YOU'VE FOUND SOME SPECTACULARLY NAMED DINOS TO STAR AS YOUR TEAM OF HEROES—AND VILLAINS!

TOWERS OVER TROUBLE-MAKERS!

STOMPING OUT TROUBLE

NAME: *Dreadnoughtus*

PRONUNCIATION: dred-NAWT-us

MEANING: "fears nothing"

This supersize sauropod was one of the largest land-dwelling animals of all time: It was 85 feet (26 m) from head to tail and weighed more than four full school buses. Scientists have documented sauropod footprints up to 5.6 feet (1.7 m) long—large enough to crush rogues, scoundrels, and all brand of bandits.

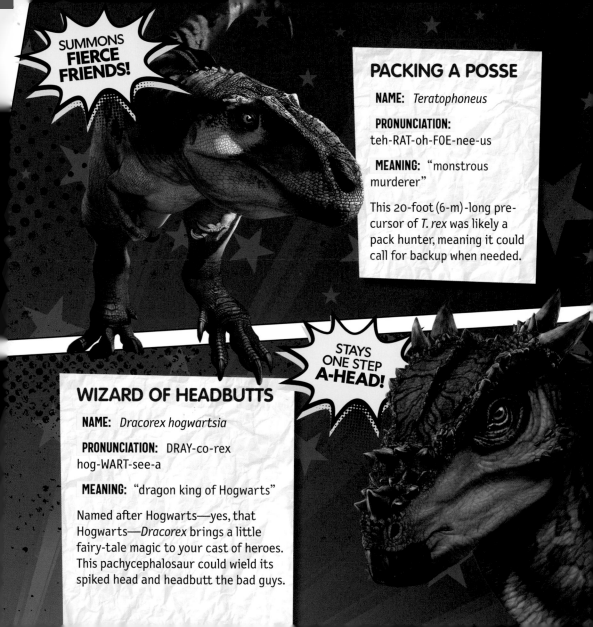

SUMMONS FIERCE FRIENDS!

PACKING A POSSE

NAME: *Teratophoneus*

PRONUNCIATION: teh-RAT-oh-FOE-nee-us

MEANING: "monstrous murderer"

This 20-foot (6-m)-long precursor of *T. rex* was likely a pack hunter, meaning it could call for backup when needed.

STAYS ONE STEP A-HEAD!

WIZARD OF HEADBUTTS

NAME: *Dracorex hogwartsia*

PRONUNCIATION: DRAY-co-rex hog-WART-see-a

MEANING: "dragon king of Hogwarts"

Named after Hogwarts—yes, that Hogwarts—*Dracorex* brings a little fairy-tale magic to your cast of heroes. This pachycephalosaur could wield its spiked head and headbutt the bad guys.

GETTING A LEG UP

LEDUMAHADI MAY HAVE BEEN ABLE TO REAR UP ON ITS BACK LEGS.

LEDUMAHADI   le-dew-ma-HAR-dee

Ledumahadi roamed the land that is now South Africa some 200 million years ago. At that time, this early Jurassic prehistoric plant-eater was the largest land animal on Earth. *Ledumahadi* was a sauropodomorph, an ancestral relative of sauropods. At about 13 tons (12 t) it was pretty hefty (about the weight of two adult African elephants!), but *Ledumahadi* didn't achieve the size of some of the sauropods (like *Argentinosaurus*) that would flourish later, during the Cretaceous. Sauropods supported their immense weight on four column-like legs (kind of like elephants!), but *Ledumahadi* managed to grow big without similarly stilt-like limbs. Though it also stood on four legs, *Ledumahadi* had more flexible limbs that could partly bend—allowing it to crouch kind of like a cat does.

AWESOME ANATOMY: BIG BONES

Dinosaurs were either bipeds (meaning they walked on two legs) or quadrupeds (meaning they walked on four legs). The researchers investigating *Ledumahadi* figured out that when animals walk just on their back limbs (bipeds), the bones of their front limbs are thinner and less substantial. But animals that walk on four legs (quadrupeds) have sturdier bones in their front limbs to help bear their weight. By comparing *Ledumahadi*'s arm and leg bones with those of other dinosaurs, they determined that *Ledumahadi* was a quadruped, like the sauropods that would come later.

151

DINO BITE

The dino's species name, *Ledumahadi mafube*, means "a giant thunderclap [at] dawn" in Southern Sotho, one of the languages spoken where its fossils were discovered.

DINO BITE

Scientists estimate that *Ledumahadi* grew to more than 30 feet (9 m) long.

DINO HIGH
CLASS SUPERLATIVES

Class Clown

Arms longer than an adult human, capped off with claws as long as forks: This is what fossil hunters found in 1965, when they first uncovered the remains of a late Cretaceous creature in the Gobi desert. A half a century later, they had uncovered enough of this unusual animal to figure out what the rest of it looked like. And it looked … pretty weird. *Deinocheirus* (whose name means "unusual terrible hand") was as tall as a giraffe and more than three times as heavy, with a long toothless snout, a pointy head, a bulging belly, and a hump on its back. This baffling beast wins the contest for class clown, (enormous) hands down.

Keep being you!
—Velociraptor

You always made me laugh!

xoxo Protoceratops ♥

Biggest Heavyweight, **pages 28–29**

Brainiest, **pages 82–83**

Super Sprinter, **pages 140–141**

Most Likely to Succeed, **pages 208–209**

TAKING WING

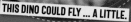

THIS DINO COULD FLY ... A LITTLE.

ARCHAEOPTERYX ark-ee-OP-turr-icks

It's a bird! It's ... not a bird? *Archaeopteryx* has been vital to our understanding of how dinosaurs evolved. The fossil remains of this hugely important find were first discovered in southern Germany in the early 1860s. Dating back to the Jurassic period, the bones were remarkable for exhibiting features of both birds and reptiles: feathers and wings, but also toothy jaws, sharp claws, and a bony tail. Known as a "transitional fossil," *Archaeopteryx* revealed evidence to scientists that modern-day birds evolved from the predatory dinosaurs known as theropods. Birds are considered "avian dinosaurs," a lineage that survived the late Cretaceous extinction.

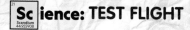

Strange Science: TEST FLIGHT

For a long time, scientists debated whether *Archaeopteryx* could fly. It had feathered wings, but could it flap them and take flight? To find out, a group of scientists used an advanced technology called phase-contrast synchrotron microtomography, which allowed them to take powerful x-rays of the narrowest, middle part of the wing bones of three *Archaeopteryx* specimens. They then compared the data they gathered to that of dozens of modern birds, as well as a couple of crocodylians and pterosaurs. In 2018, scientists announced that their study of the front limb bones of *Archaeopteryx* revealed it was most similar to the wing bones of quails and pheasants, birds that can fly for short distances.

DINO BITE

Archaeopteryx probably used its claws to climb up trees and then glide down.

DINO BITE

Archaeopteryx was about the size of a pigeon and had jet-black feathers, like a raven.

BLACK FEATHERS? HOW IN THE WORLD DID SCIENTISTS FIGURE THAT ONE OUT? CHECK OUT THE ANSWER ON THE NEXT PAGE!

155

FAQ WHAT COLOR WERE DINOSAURS?

Books and movies usually depict dinosaurs as dull-colored creatures in shades of green, gray, and brown. But were these their real colors? And how do we know?

While bones can turn into fossils that last for millions of years, skin rarely fossilizes. So for a long time, scientists were just guessing about dinosaurs' colors. But then, in 2008, a team at Yale University made an amazing discovery: They peered inside a fossilized feather and found melanosomes, pigment-filled sacs that give living cells their color. By comparing the preserved melanosomes to those in the feathers of living birds, the scientists could figure out what color the ancient flier had been. It was a new way to determine the color of feathered dinosaurs.

Before long, scientists had uncovered the colors of all sorts of dinos. There was *Anchiornis huxleyi*, with bold striped black-and-white wings and a bright red mohawk on its head. There was *Caihong juji*, which sported a head and chest covered with glittering iridescent rainbow feathers, like those of a modern hummingbird. Of course, not all dinos came in bright hues: *Sinosauropteryx* used a mix of dark and light shades to camouflage itself against the prehistoric landscape.

DINO BITE

Microraptor had shiny blue-black feathers similar to those of a modern crow.

DINO BITE

Scientists believe that dinosaurs with brightly colored feathers probably used them to attract mates and intimidate rivals, just like modern birds.

SINOSAUROPTERYX

ANCIENT ANIMAL ART

FOR CENTURIES, PEOPLE HAVE RELIED ON ARTISTS TO TURN FOSSILS INTO IMAGES OF FLESH-AND-BLOOD CREATURES. THESE ARTISTS HAVE USUALLY (THOUGH NOT ALWAYS!) BASED THEIR DEPICTIONS ON THE BEST FOSSIL EVIDENCE AND THE SCIENTIFIC KNOWLEDGE AVAILABLE AT THE TIME. THERE'S ONLY ONE PROBLEM—WHAT WE KNOW ABOUT DINOSAURS KEEPS CHANGING!

THE UNDERWATER SCUFFLE

In 1830, geologist and paleontologist Henry Thomas De la Beche was the first person known to create a piece of paleoart (art depicting prehistoric life). To bring attention to the work of his friend and neighbor, a famed fossil hunter named Mary Anning (p. 104), he painted "Duria Antiquior—A More Ancient Dorset." The watercolor depicted a vivid scene of prehistoric creatures battling each other, including ichthyosaurs and plesiosaurs, two of Anning's notable finds. Today, we know that it's unlikely these creatures would have ever battled in real life.

THE PREHISTORIC PARK

In the early 1850s, a British naturalist and artist named Benjamin Waterhouse Hawkins was hired to create life-size sculptures for a prehistoric park in London, England. His sculptures, which were based on the fossil information gathered by scientists up to that point, were the first time dinosaurs had been seen by a wide audience. Although we now know that the replicas aren't accurate, these ancient animals—which included *Iguanodon*, *Hylaeosaurus*, *Ichthyosaurus*, *Pterodactylus*, and *Megalosaurus*—are still on display in Crystal Palace Park, in the south of London.

THE HOLLYWOOD TREATMENT

Scientists didn't know that many dinosaurs had feathers until the late 1990s—after scaly dinos had already become pop culture icons. Today, most movies still portray dinos as leathery reptilians. Hollywood's historical preference to keep their supersize stars super scaly has influenced how most people have traditionally pictured dinosaurs.

CREATING ACCURATE ART OF ANIMALS NO ONE HAS EVER SEEN IN THE FLESH IS A TOUGH JOB! FORTUNATELY, THE DINO PRO ON THE NEXT PAGE IS TACKLING THE TASK.

DINO PRO:
JULIUS CSOTONYI

Want to see a *T. rex* hunting its dinner near a coastal swamp? What about a *Brachiosaurus* lumbering along at dawn in a Jurassic forest? Or a pterosaur swooping along the water's surface to scoop up a seafood dinner?

Not possible, we know. The closest you'll get to seeing these animals in their ancient ecosystems is Julius Csotonyi's art, which takes us back in time by making long-extinct animals and their environments come alive. Paleoartists like Csotonyi use information from what scientists have written to make their work as realistic as possible. They use a combination of what we know for sure from fossil evidence and what we know about other (living) animals to fill in missing pieces (such as what color an animal may have been). Csotonyi's goal is to make sure his depictions of dinosaurs and other prehistoric creatures walking, swimming, and flying in ancient landscapes are both awe-inspiring and realistic.

Csotonyi, who is based in Vancouver, Canada, has created life-size dinosaur murals for Canada's Royal Ontario Museum and the Natural History Museum in Los Angeles. For the renovated fossil hall at the Smithsonian National Museum of Natural History in Washington, D.C., he digitally painted 59 pieces. Many pieces of his art were published in a book called *The Paleoart of Julius Csotonyi*, and he has even made his mark on money: Csotonyi made photorealistic illustrations of *T. rex* for U.S. postage stamps and created dinos on collectible glow-in-the-dark coins issued by the Royal Canadian Mint.

"I became interested in drawing dinosaurs as a kid, as do many kids. I never grew out of my 'dinophile' phase."

JULIUS CSOTONYI

Csotonyi creating a digital painting

A REAL GEM

WEEWARRASAURUS
WEE-wahr-rah-SORE-us

Everything scientists know about this dino they learned from its lower jaw. And what an amazing jaw it was: The fossil fragment of *Weewarrasaurus pobeni*'s jawbone was found preserved in shimmering green-and-blue opal, a precious gemstone. It was unearthed from a mine near the town of Lightning Ridge, New South Wales, Australia, part of the Australian outback. Though this area is now dry and dusty, when *Weewarrasaurus pobeni* roamed it, about 100 million years ago, the landscape was very different. At that time, it was filled with lush forests and waterways that drained into an ancient seaway known as the Eromanga Sea. *Weewarrasaurus pobeni* was a member of a group of plant-eating dinosaurs known as ornithopods. It moved on two legs across the ancient flood plains of Cretaceous-period eastern Australia, using its beak and teeth to munch on low branches and eat plants that grew around the area's rivers, lakes, and lagoons.

THE FOSSIL PRESERVED IN OPAL

A Gem of a Find

Weewarrasaurus pobeni takes its genus name from where it was found: the Wee Warra opal field. Its species name is in recognition of Mike Poben, an Australian opal buyer. In 2013, Poben bought a couple of bags of rough opal from miners in the Lightning Ridge area. As he picked through the bags for fossils, as he always did, he spotted something unusual: Poben noticed a couple of scallop-shaped ridges in the shimmering stone and immediately knew this was no ordinary piece of stone. "A voice in the back of my head said, teeth," he said. "I thought ... if I have teeth here, then this is a jawbone."

FANTASTIC FOSSILS

OVER THE YEARS, SCIENTISTS HAVE UNEARTHED LOTS OF INCREDIBLE EVIDENCE SHOWING THE WAY DINOSAURS LOOKED AND BEHAVED. HERE ARE A FEW OF THEIR MOST FUNDAMENTAL FINDS.

THE FIRST FEMUR

In the late 1600s, a university professor discovered a huge femur (thigh bone) near Oxford, England. At that time, no one had even heard of "dinosaurs." Was it from a giant reptile? Or from some other oversize animal? It wasn't until 1824 that a British geologist named William Buckland identified the very first dinosaur ever to be recognized by science: Jurassic-period predator *Megalosaurus.*

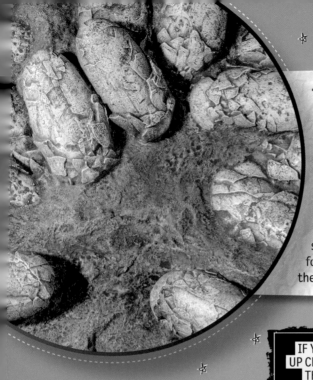

THE BEST NEST

Now that's a full house! A full nest of 15 *Protoceratops* babies was unearthed in the Gobi desert, Mongolia, in 2011. Smaller than the length of a pencil, the young dinos were probably a year old, at most, when they were suddenly buried by a sandstorm. The discovery of so many young dinos of the same size in the same nest suggests that *Protoceratops* may have cared for their young for an extended period after they hatched.

IF YOU WISH YOU COULD SEE THE "DUELING DINOS" UP CLOSE AND PERSONAL, YOU'LL WANT TO CHECK OUT THE WORK OF THE DINO PRO ON THE NEXT PAGE.

THE "DUELING DINOSAURS"

It must have been quite a scuffle! Around 67 million years ago, a *T. rex* and a *Triceratops* were buried suddenly—side by side and intertwined mid-tussle—on a coastal plain in what is now Montana, U.S.A. Their swift burial meant this iconic moment would be well-preserved: This fossil, which was discovered in 2006, contains skeletons among the most complete ever discovered of each of these well-known dinos.

**DINO PRO:
LINDSAY ZANNO**

Paleontologist

Lindsay Zanno is part of the team developing the "Dueling Dinosaurs" exhibit at the North Carolina Museum of Natural Sciences. Scheduled to open in 2023, the exhibit will not only feature the fossils but will allow the public to observe the museum's team of scientists performing actual research on the specimens in the Zanno lab. It will also feature a public lab, where visitors can re-create the science they are observing.

Zanno has spent years performing fieldwork at dig sites around the world, looking for and collecting fossils of dinosaurs and other Mesozoic vertebrates. She has discovered more than a dozen new species, including *Siats meekerorum*, one of the largest carnivorous dinos ever unearthed in North America, and *Moros intrepidus*, the oldest Cretaceous tyrannosaur found so far in North America. Zanno is an expert on theropods, a group of dinos that includes ultra-famous feathered predators *Velociraptor* and *T. rex.*

When she's not on expeditions, Zanno makes it her mission to teach and train young scientists and get the public excited about dinosaurs, through both her job as head of paleontology at the museum and her position as an associate research professor at North Carolina State University.

> "A lot of what I do involves fieldwork, which is probably the thing I love the most about my job."
>
> **LINDSAY ZANNO**

Zanno in the field

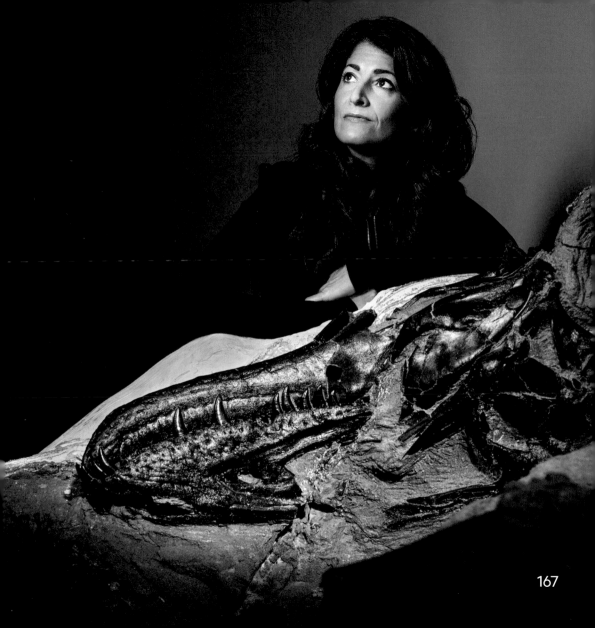

A FIND WITH TEETH

AQUILOPS AMERICANUS
ACK-will-ops a-MER-uh-KA-nus

Bunny-size and bird-faced: That was *Aquilops americanus*, the earliest known horned dinosaur from North America. It was discovered in 1997, when scientists on an expedition in Montana, U.S.A., found a rock with some teeny teeth sticking out of it. The rock, which dated back about 106 million years, contained the small skull of a ceratopsian—the group of horned dinosaurs that includes the much better known *Triceratops*. Unlike *Triceratops*, which evolved tens of millions of years later, *Aquilops* did not have the trademark frill that we imagine when we think of horned dinos. It did, however, have small horns and a strongly hooked beak, which it used to dig into early Cretaceous vegetation.

DINO BITE

Aquilops had a skull about the size of a lemon.

DINO BITE

Aquilops americanus means "American eagle face."

DIGGING IT: FAR FROM HOME

Aquilops is actually more closely related to horned dinosaurs whose fossil remains have been discovered in Asia than to those uncovered in North America, where it was found. Scientists theorize that dinosaurs used a land bridge (which no longer exists) between present-day Siberia, in Northern Asia, and Alaska to migrate between Asia and North America during the Cretaceous period. The fossil record tells us that ceratopsians first evolved in Asia and crossed to North America about 108 million years ago—right around the time of *Aquilops*.

169

DESTINATION DINO: ZIGONG DINOSAUR MUSEUM

DIG IN!

Full-scale skeletons, well-preserved fossils, and interactive exhibits make this natural history museum in southwest China's Sichuan Province a destination for dinosaur lovers. Its collection contains many dinosaurs from the Jurassic period, with one of the biggest collections in the world of dinosaur fossils from that time. But what makes the Zigong Dinosaur Museum next-level amazing is its unique location: It was built on a huge exposed site filled with dinosaur fossils. Visitors inside the museum can observe firsthand an open dig site where 150-million-year-old fossils have been excavated and still lay embedded in the earth. The museum also features fossils of a variety of other ancient reptiles, as well as prehistoric fish, amphibians, and mammals.

1 Try to arrive early in the day to avoid the crowds.

2 Make sure you can spend at least two or three hours there.

TIPS FOR A GREAT VISIT:

3 Absolutely don't miss the up-close-and-personal fossil burial site!

4 Leave time to explore the grounds, including the outdoor life-size dinosaur reconstructions in the gardens.

MIGHTY MASH-UP

PEGOMASTAX   peg-OH-MAST-ax

Imagine a parrot with fangs crashing into a porcupine. That might give you some idea of what *Pegomastax* looked like. This pint-size, quill-covered reptile scurried on two legs about 200 million years ago in what is now South Africa. *Pegomastax* had large eye sockets in its skull. This attribute tells scientists that *Pegomastax*—also known as the "Dracula Dino"—may have been nocturnal, needing big eyes to see in the dark. It may have looked pretty fierce (and weird), but its diet was likely dominated by nuts, seeds, and fruit.

AWESOME ANATOMY: STRANGE SNAPPERS

It's pretty unusual for plant-eating animals to have sharp canine teeth, as *Pegomastax* did. If it didn't use them for subduing and chomping down on prey, why did it need them at all? Scientists think it may have used them for self-defense, for battling other members of its species for mates, or both. *Pegomastax* used another set of teeth in the back of its mouth for eating: Set in its upper and lower jaw, they worked like scissors—well suited for slicing up fruit.

DINO BITE

Pegomastax was only ankle-high and weighed less than a house cat.

UNEARTHING GRAVEYARDS

SCIENTISTS HAVE FOUND THE REMAINS OF PREHISTORIC ANIMALS ALL OVER THE WORLD. SOMETIMES, THEY'LL FIND *A LOT* OF FOSSILS IN ONE SPOT; THESE SITES HAVE BECOME KNOWN AS DINOSAUR GRAVEYARDS. HOW DID IT HAPPEN? LET'S VISIT A FEW AND FIND OUT.

ALBERTA, CANADA

It might be the world's largest dino graveyard. Around 76 million years ago, in what is now northern Alberta, Canada, a herd of horned dinosaurs called centrosaurs were in the wrong place at the wrong time when they were drowned in a flood caused by a huge hurricane-like storm. Scientists have found thousands of bones in the area, which stretches about 570 acres (230 ha). They estimate that the waters in what was once a coastal lowland could have risen as high as 15 feet (4.6 m), giving the dinos no way to escape.

QHEMEGA, SOUTH AFRICA

In Qhemega, located in the mountains of eastern South Africa, a shepherd named Dumangwe Thyobeka came across something amazing: a very large bone. The dinosaur graveyard it came from is believed to contain hundreds of fossils from at least a dozen different species of sauropods and their earlier relatives dating back 200 million years. How did they all wind up there? Though today it is very dry, at that time the area was filled with winding rivers. Animals that died in the rivers or on their banks would have been buried in sediment before they began to decompose.

GRAND STAIRCASE-ESCALANTE NATIONAL MONUMENT, UTAH, U.S.A.

A fantastically abundant fossil site inside Utah's Grand Staircase-Escalante National Monument was nicknamed the "Rainbows and Unicorns Quarry" because the paleontologists who excavated it were so happy to have found it. It was the final resting place of several tyrannosaurs, as well as other dinos, turtles, and an alligator the length of two refrigerators. The prehistoric creatures are believed to have met their collective end during a flood, which washed their remains into a lake.

KIND OF A STRETCH

BRACHIOSAURUS   BRAK-ee-oh-SORE-us

Talk about sticking your neck out! Like other sauropods, *Brachiosaurus* had a superlong neck and a head that looked a little too small for its body. But what made *Brachiosaurus* stand out from the pack was its immense reach: It could hold its tall neck directly upright, allowing it to access leaves about four stories high! Weighing between 33 and 55 tons (30 to 50 t)—about the heft of a dozen African elephants—it lumbered around on four legs during the late Jurassic, using its spoon-shaped teeth to graze on treetops in what is now the western United States. To gain enough energy to haul itself around, this hungry herbivore needed to eat constantly—hundreds of pounds of vegetation a day!

AWESOME ANATOMY: HEAD HELD HIGH

Brachiosaurus's neck stretched 30 feet (9 m) long— about five times as long as a giraffe's! How did *Brachiosaurus* and other sauropods support these extended appendages? There were hollow areas in sauropods' vertebrae (neck bones) that held air-filled sacs. This would have made their lengthy necks much lighter, allowing them to both hold up their necks and maneuver them around.

DINO BITE

Brachiosaurus had a bulge on its head that worked like nostrils, providing an airway that allowed the dinosaur to breathe while it ate.

DINO BITE

Brachiosaurus means "arm lizard," a name that comes from its front legs being longer than its back ones. Its front legs carried most of its weight.

177

Cretaceous Comics presents ...

AWARD-WINNING OOPS!

I'M STILL ON DISPLAY—AND I'VE GOT MY (CORRECT) HEAD SCREWED ON STRAIGHT NOW!

IMAGINE YOU ARE A PRESENTER AT "THE GOLDEN DINOS," SELECTED TO GIVE OUT THE "OOPS, THAT DOESN'T GO THERE!" AWARD. THE NOMINEES ARE ...

APATOSAURUS

From 1934 to 1979, the Carnegie Museum in Pittsburgh, Pennsylvania, U.S.A., displayed its huge *Apatosaurus* skeleton with ... the head of an entirely different dinosaur: *Camarasaurus*.

I'M A MARINE REPTILE, NOT A DINO. BUT DOESN'T THIS **SUPER-STRANGE SWAP** EARN ME A PLACE IN THE LINEUP?

ELASMOSAURUS

In 1868, an *Elasmosaurus* skeleton was reconstructed with its head on its tail ... instead of its neck.

IGUANODON

When it was originally reconstructed, in the early 19th century, *Iguanodon*'s thumb spike was placed on its nose ... kind of like a rhinoceros.

TO BE FAIR, **I WAS ONE OF THE FIRST DINOS EVER DISCOVERED.** SCIENTISTS WERE STILL FIGURING IT OUT!

BECOMING A FOSSIL

HOW DO WE KNOW SO MUCH ABOUT DINOSAURS? FOSSILS ARE A HUGE REASON. SCIENTISTS CAN LEARN WHEN AN ANIMAL LIVED, HOW IT LOOKED, OR WHAT IT ATE BY STUDYING THEM. BUT HOW DOES AN ANIMAL BECOME A FOSSIL?

STEP 1:
THE END

An animal meets its end. The soft parts of its body, such as its tissues, decompose or are scavenged by other animals. The hard parts of the animal, such as its bones, shell, or teeth, are left. If mud, soil, silt, or sand rapidly bury these hard remains, there is a possibility this creature will become a fossil.

STEP 2:

GET BURIED

Over time, more and more (and more) layers of sediment form on top of the animal's hard remains, burying them deeper and deeper under dirt and rock. Increased pressure turns the lower layers into hard rock. The animal's skeleton is eventually dissolved by groundwater, leaving an empty space in the rock in the shape of the original bones.

STEP 3:

TIME PASSES

During the course of millions and millions of years, minerals from the ground, lakes, or oceans enter this empty space and fill it, forming a "cast" in the same shape of the original bones. This process, called permineralization, is the most common type of fossil preservation.

STEP 4:

FEELING EXPOSED

More time passes. The shifting of Earth's plates in natural events such as earthquakes eventually move the fossilized remains closer to Earth's surface. The process of erosion by wind and rain exposes the fossils, where they are discovered by scientists, amateur fossil hunters, or others. Many fossils are discovered in areas that were once covered by water.

DOUBLE-CRESTED PREDATOR

DILOPHOSAURUS di-LOWF-oh-SORE-us

Only about twice the length of a Ping-Pong table, the early Jurassic theropod *Dilophosaurus* wasn't one of the hugest dinos that ever lived. But when it roamed what is now the American Southwest about 193 million years ago, it was a pretty sizable predator—so sizable, actually, that it was the largest known land animal to have lived in North America by that time. *Dilophosaurus* was much bigger than the carnivorous dinos that had come before it, and it was a preview of the enormous theropods that would evolve later: Its distant cousin *T. rex*, which lived during the Cretaceous period, was twice its length and 15 times its weight.

DINO BITE

Fossilized tracks found in Utah, U.S.A., suggest that *Dilophosaurus* sat like a modern-day bird.

AWESOME ANATOMY: COOL CRESTS

Dilophosaurus **had a pretty unusual head.** Two bony, parallel crests sat atop its snout, possibly there to lure potential mates or to help the dino regulate its body temperature. Scientists believe the crests were probably covered in keratin (or skin with keratin in it), similar to the head crests of some modern birds, such as the cassowary. (Keratin is the same protein that's in your fingernails and hair.) *Dilophosaurus* means "two-crested lizard," owing to its half-moon-shaped headgear.

WHICH
DINO
PROFESSION
WOULD YOU CHOOSE?

IF YOU DIG DINOS AND OTHER PREHISTORIC ANIMALS (OR PLANTS!), THERE ARE LOTS OF COOL JOBS OUT THERE TO EXPLORE. TAKE THIS QUIZ TO GET AN IDEA WHAT PROFESSION WORKS FOR YOU!

•START HERE•

DO YOU LIKE TO BE OUTSIDE?

I prefer to be indoors... but not all the time!

DO YOU WANT TO MOSTLY HANDLE ARTIFACTS OR MOSTLY MAKE ART?

Art!

Artifacts!

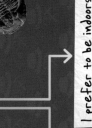

I live for the great outdoors.

WANT TO STUDY WHAT'S LEFT OF ANIMALS, OR WHAT ANIMALS LEFT BEHIND?

I want to follow the footprints.

Animal remains, all day.

BACKBONES OR NO BACKBONES?

184

PALEOARTISTS
draw and/or sculpt prehistoric animals for books, scientific articles, and museums.

MUSEUM CURATORS
create and help assemble exhibitions about dinos and prehistoric life.

ICHNOLOGISTS
study fossilized tracks, footprints, nests, burrows—traces of what prehistoric creatures did while they were alive.

The more bones the better!

VERTEBRATE PALEONTOLOGISTS
study fossils of animals with backbones, like dinosaurs, pterosaurs, and crocodiles, to show what they looked like and how they lived.

Spineless, please.

INVERTEBRATE PALEONTOLOGISTS
study the fossils of animals without backbones, such as worms, sponges, mollusks, and corals.

HELMET HEAD

CORYTHOSAURUS **koh-rith-OH-sore-us**

Many *Corythosaurus* **skeletons**—both juvenile and adult— have been discovered over the years. Because of these abundant and complete fossil finds, *Corythosaurus* is one of the dinosaurs best known to science. About half the length of a bowling lane, *Corythosaurus* was one of the larger members of the hadrosaurid (duck-billed dino) family. A distinctive ridge formed by tall bony spines covered with skin ran along its back, and it had a prominent crest above its eyes. It walked and ran on two legs foraging for leaves and fruits in warm woodlands approximately 75 million years ago.

AWESOME ANATOMY: SOUNDING IT OUT

Over the years, scientists have had different theories about what *Corythosaurus*'s impressive headgear was used for. Did the hollow crest, which is connected to tubes in its nostrils, sharpen the animal's sense of smell? Was the crest an air tank that allowed it to breathe underwater? Most scientists believe the crest allowed *Corythosaurus* to communicate by making loud sounds over long distances, either to attract mates or as a way to warn its pack about approaching predators.

DINO BITE

Fossilized skin impressions of *Corythosaurus* have been found, revealing that it had wartlike lumps on its belly.

DINO BITE

This hadrosaur earned its name—which means "helmet lizard"—owing to its platelike crest.

WHAT DID DINOSAURS SOUND LIKE? FIND THE ANSWERS ON THE NEXT PAGE.

 **FAQ** DID DINOSAURS ROAR?

You've seen it in the movies: A dinosaur opens its huge, toothy, menacing mouth and lets out an earthshaking *ROOOAAARRR!* But, like a lot of what we see in made-up movies about dinosaurs, this is probably pure fiction. Scientists aren't entirely certain what dino sounds echoed throughout the Mesozoic. But they're pretty sure dinos likely didn't roar the way we think of roaring—the way lions, tigers, and bears do.

Instead of vocalizing with their mouths open, many dinosaurs may have made noises through something called "closed-mouth vocalizations." Modern-day animals produce these kinds of sounds by inflating their esophagus or the pouches on their windpipe. This produces a low-pitched sound, like the cooing you'd hear from a pigeon, the growl you'd hear from a crocodile, or the "booms" you may have heard from an ostrich. Because the organs that dinosaurs would have used to make these sounds were made of soft tissue, they did not fossilize (that is, there's no specific fossil evidence for this ... yet). This makes it challenging for scientists to understand what dinosaur vocalizations may have sounded like. They can learn more by studying the anatomy of modern animals and comparing it to what they do know about dinos.

DINO BITE

Dinos may have also made noises by *swooshing* their tails, the way modern-day reptiles do.

DINO BITE

Duck-billed dinos sported hollow crests with long nasal passages. When air was blown through, it would have produced low, foghorn-like sounds.

The mighty roar of the *T. rex* in *Jurassic Park* was a remixed combination of baby elephant squealing, tiger snarling, and alligator gurgling.

FOSSILS FOUND ...
WHERE?

FOSSILS OF PREHISTORIC ANIMALS HAVE BEEN DISCOVERED ALL OVER THE WORLD. SOMETIMES THEY TURN UP IN PLACES WE MIGHT NOT HAVE EXPECTED THEM!

AT A CONSTRUCTION SITE

In August 2017, a construction crew building a new public safety facility in Thornton, Colorado, U.S.A., noticed something unusual sticking up through the ground. It looked like a bone! After brushing off the dirt and getting a closer look, they called the Denver Museum of Nature and Science. At first, scientists thought the 66-million-year-old fossil belonged to a *Triceratops*. But after excavating and studying more of the skeleton, scientists determined it was actually *Torosaurus*, a close cousin of *Triceratops*. This was the first recorded *Torosaurus* find in Colorado!

NEAR A PARKING LOT

In 2012, after dropping his wife at work at NASA's Goddard Space Flight Center in Greenbelt, Maryland, U.S.A., amateur paleontologist Ray Stanford noticed a cool chunk of rock jutting out of the grass on a hill near the parking lot. It turned out this 8.5-foot (2.6-m), 100-million-year-old slab of sandstone contained a collection of about 70 fossilized tracks from eight different species of mammals and dinosaurs, including theropods, nodosaurs, and a sauropod.

BEHIND A MALL

Inversand quarry is a fossil dig site behind a shopping mall in Mantua Township, New Jersey, U.S.A. (yes, a shopping mall!). Scientists believe the "mass death assemblage" of mosasaur fossils they discovered 40 feet (12.2 m) beneath the surface there were killed as a result of the asteroid that struck Earth (p. 206) about 66 million years ago. Though billions of animals died as a result of this cataclysmic collision, scientists rarely find the remains of any of them. If these mosasaurs (marine reptiles) did meet their end as a result of that extreme extinction event, their fossils would give scientists important information about that period of Earth's history.

CHUNKY CHOMPERS

IGUANODON   ih-GWAHN-oh-don

First discovered in the 1820s in Sussex, England, the earliest remains of this heavy herbivore came in the form of some very large teeth. Can you guess why, a few years later, doctor and amateur fossil collector Gideon Mantell gave the owner of these curious chompers a name that means "iguana teeth"? Yup—*Iguanodon*'s teeth looked like those of an iguana, only much, much (much!) bigger—about 20 times bigger. And it had about 100 of them, which it used to munch on tree leaves and low-growing vegetation that it tore off with its sharp beak. *Iguanodon* wandered through woodlands in what is now western Europe around 125 million years ago, mostly on its four solid legs. Its hind legs were larger and stronger than its front legs and had three thick toes that were likely padded, allowing it to more comfortably carry around its three-ton (2.7-t) body when it stood or walked (or ran!) on two feet.

AWESOME ANATOMY: DYNAMIC DIGITS

Iguanodon **had a pretty interesting hand:** three middle fingers, with a little finger on one side and a spiked thumb on the other. It could curl its little finger across its palm to grab food and use its thumb spike to, well … do a few different things. This sharp digit could have been wielded as a weapon in close combat with theropods, either as defense against predators or when brawling with rival dinos of its own species. It might have also used its thumb spike to cut plants or crack into seeds and fruits.

DINO BITE

Iguanodon was only the second dinosaur to be scientifically named. (*Megalosaurus* was the first.)

DINO BITE

Iguanodon is part of the group known as iguanodontians, which also includes the hadrosaurs (duck-billed dinosaurs).

BENE-FISH-AL FEATURES

BARYONYX BAH-ree-ON-icks

Like other spinosaurids, *Baryonyx* had attributes that suggest it was a strong hunter on both land *and* in the water: hands with three sharp claws, powerful arms, and crocodile-like jaws and teeth. Because its nostrils were positioned back from the tip of its long snout, and because it had a curved upper jaw, *Baryonyx* probably thrust its head into the water to snap up aquatic animals. *Baryonyx* may have crouched next to rivers, waiting to strike, or even waded into water to find its dinner. It feasted on both supersize fish and other dinosaurs—including *Iguanodon*—125 million years ago in what is now Europe and western Africa. *Baryonyx* weighed more than a ton (1.1 t) and grew to be about 30 feet (9 m) long.

A FOSSIL OF THE PREHISTORIC FISH *LEPIDOTES*

ON THE MENU: BIG FISH

A favorite food of *Baryonyx* was a bony fish called *Lepidotes* (leppy-DOE-tees), which could grow up to six feet (1.8 m) long. Scientists know this because both bones and scales of *Lepidotes* have been found in the fossilized stomach remains of *Baryonyx*. *Lepidotes,* which was covered in thick, glossy-looking scales, inhabited lakes in the Northern Hemisphere between 199 and 70 million years ago.

DINO BITE

Baryonyx had 96 serrated (knifelike) teeth in its long jaw, twice as many as some other spinosaurids.

DINO BITE

Baryonyx means "heavy claw," owing to the 12-inch (31-cm) thumb-like claws it could use to hook fish.

WINGING IT

CAUDIPTERYX   caw-DIP-ter-ix

If you had spotted *Caudipteryx* walking around during the early Cretaceous period, you might have thought it was a bird. About the size of a peacock, it was covered in feathers, with a fan of long feathers at the end of its tail and on its forearms. These winglike arms, however, were too short for *Caudipteryx* to have been able to use them to fly; it more likely used them to attract mates or to keep warm. *Caudipteryx* was, in fact, not at all a bird—not even a flightless bird. It was an oviraptorosaur, a family of birdlike dinos with parrotlike beaks whose remains have been found in what is today Asia and North America. When *Caudipteryx* was first found, in western Liaoning Province, China, in the late 1990s, it was one of the first known feathered dinosaurs.

ON THE MENU: A DIVERSE DIET

Caudipteryx **was thought to have been an omnivore,** meaning that its diet included both animals and plants. The dino's remains were found along with gastroliths, small stones that birds swallow and keep in their gizzards (stomach) to grind up food such as plants. But *Caudipteryx* also had sharp teeth and long legs that it could have used to move quickly, which means it may have also been a hunter.

196

197

DESTINATION DINO: CLEVELAND–LLOYD DINOSAUR QUARRY

POWER IN NUMBERS

Here's a head-scratcher: How did more than 12,000 bones from 74 individual dinosaurs wind up in one place? That's a lot of bones! And it's still mostly a mystery for the paleontologists who have been excavating these fossils from the Cleveland-Lloyd Dinosaur Quarry since the 1920s. The site, located at Jurassic National Monument in east-central Utah, U.S.A., has the most concentrated number of dino bones from the Jurassic period ever discovered in one place. Most of the bones that scientists have unearthed (dating back between 148 and 146 million years ago) have come from meat-eaters—one predator in particular: *Allosaurus*, the top carnivore in North America during the late Jurassic. Forty-six individual *Allosaurus* specimens—ranging in size from 10 to 40 feet (3–12 m)— have been found at the Quarry. It's no wonder *Allosaurus* is the state fossil of Utah!

1 The Cleveland–Lloyd Dinosaur Quarry is open only seasonally (in the spring, summer, and fall) and on certain days of the week, so plan your visit accordingly.

2 Temperatures in Utah can reach more than 100°F (38°C)! Apply sunscreen, wear a hat, and always bring along enough water.

TIPS FOR A GREAT VISIT:

3 This is an active dig site! Keep your eyes peeled for bones as you hike along the site's trails.

4 Take a break from the heat and check out the *Allosaurus* exhibit in the visitor center.

HAVE YOU HERD

MUSSAURUS moos-SORE-us

Paleontologists have known for a while that dinosaurs created nesting grounds and lived in herds. But a discovery in the Laguna Colorada Formation in Patagonia, Argentina, showed them that dinosaurs had been hanging out in packs much earlier than they thought—about 40 million years earlier! Scientists unearthed a 193-million-year-old dinosaur nesting ground filled with fossilized eggs, nests, and dozens of newborn, juvenile, and adult skeletons of *Mussaurus patagonicus,* an early sauropod dinosaur. The range in ages from embryo to fully grown adult found all in one site suggests to scientists that *Mussaurus* formed communal breeding grounds. Further, scientists saw that *Mussaurus* fossils of a similar age were buried together at the site: eggs and hatchlings in one area, young dinos in another, and adults alone or in pairs. This likely means that the younger *Mussaurus* stayed together while the adults went out to forage for food—similar to the multifamily, lifelong herds we see in modern-day animals such as elephants.

Strange Science:

EGG-CELLENT X-RAY

A team of scientists excavated and studied the bones of 80 juvenile and adult *Mussaurus*, along with more than 100 dinosaur eggs. How could they have known that what was inside the eggs were also *Mussaurus*? To "see" inside the dinosaur eggs, they used x-ray tomography imaging, a technology that allows scientists to view what is inside solid objects without breaking them open. Using this technology, they could "see" the preserved dino embryos inside the eggs and confirm that they were indeed also developing *Mussaurus*.

DINO BITE

Mussaurus eggs were about the size of chicken eggs.

SHORT AND STUBBY

GUEMESIA   gweh-MEH-see-uh

About 70 million years ago, a big dinosaur with tiny arms lived in what is today northern Argentina. That's where scientists found the upper and back parts of the skull (known as the braincase) of *Guemesia ochoai,* a member of a family of meat-eating dinosaurs known as abelisaurids. This family flourished during the Cretaceous period, roaming the supercontinent Gondwana. Abelisaurids were top predators, ferocious and strong enough to have preyed on even the biggest dinos of all time: the titanosaurs. And they managed to do it with arms even smaller than *T. rex*'s! How did *Guemesia* successfully hunt its dinner with such short and stubby arms? *Guemesia* had a hard head, which it may have used to ram its prey, along with powerful jaws and a sharp sense of smell.

AWESOME ANATOMY: LEFTOVERS

Guemesia **probably had partially vestigial arms,** meaning its forelimbs were basically useless. Vestigial body parts are parts of a creature's anatomy that were once useful to its ancestors, but, as a result of being used less and less, became smaller or less functional as the species evolved. Even humans have vestigial body parts: Your tailbone and wisdom teeth are both vestigial!

DINO BITE

Guemesia had a much smaller braincase than other abelisaurids. It was only 70 percent the size of *Carnotaurus*'s!

FANTASTIC FIRSTS

SPICOMELLUS **SPY-co-MEL-us**

Up until the discovery of *Spicomellus*, ankylosaurs had only ever been found in North America. *Spicomellus*, which was discovered in the Middle Atlas mountains in Morocco, is the first ever ankylosaur found on the African continent. But that wasn't its only first: *Spicomellus* is also the first dino ever found to have defensive spikes attached to its skeleton instead of to its skin, as they are connected in other armored dinosaurs. *Spicomellus* dates back around 168 million years, making it the oldest ankylosaur ever discovered.

A *SPICOMELLUS* TAIL SPIKE

AWESOME ANATOMY:

THE RIB BONE'S CONNECTED TO THE ... WHAT?

Scientists know what they do about *Spicomellus* from only one part of the animal: a section of its ribs. Fused to the surface of the dorsal (back) rib specimen is an osteoderm (a piece of armor plate) with four spikes attached. In other armored dinos, the rib bones were covered by a layer of muscle and then by skin, with the spikes embedded in that. But *Spicomellus*'s armor is connected directly to its rib bones—a structure that scientists have never before seen in any other vertebrate, either living or extinct. Now that's a first!

DINO BITE

Spicomellus means "collar of spikes."

DINO BITE

Spicomellus was discovered by a farmer at the same site where, a couple of years earlier, scientists had unearthed *Adratiklit*, the oldest stegosaur ever found.

SOMETIMES YOU'RE FIRST, AND SOMETIMES YOU'RE LAST. TURN THE PAGE TO LEARN ABOUT THE END OF THE AGE OF DINOS.

FAQ HOW DID DINOSAURS BECOME EXTINCT?

Most experts now agree that the age of dinosaurs ended about 66 million years ago, when an asteroid nearly nine miles (14.4 km) wide careened into the waters off the coast of what is now Mexico—causing a massive storm of rock and glass, as well as tsunamis and forest fires carried by hurricane-force winds, that reached more than 2,100 miles (3,500 km) from the impact site. Animals that did not die in the immediate aftermath of the asteroid eventually succumbed to other catastrophic consequences: toxic air, acid rain, and climate change. Volcanic eruptions spewed dangerous chemicals into the air, as well as soot so thick it blocked out the sun. Both on land and in the sea, plants that relied on the sun died. With nothing to eat, the animals that ate those plants—and the animals that ate those animals—also died. Because the asteroid had slammed into rocks that contained a large amount of carbonates, immense quantities of carbon dioxide were released into the air. Carbon dioxide traps heat, which creates a kind of blanket over Earth. This caused Earth's temperatures to rise by about nine degrees Fahrenheit (5 degrees Celsius)—an increase that lasted for 100,000 years! It is estimated to have taken thousands of years for Earth to see the full extent of the global extinction, which wiped out three-quarters of Earth's land, air, and sea creatures—including the dino-saurs. (Though not all the dinos! Turn the page for more.)

DINO BITE

Scientists believe the asteroid most likely struck during what was springtime in the Northern Hemisphere.

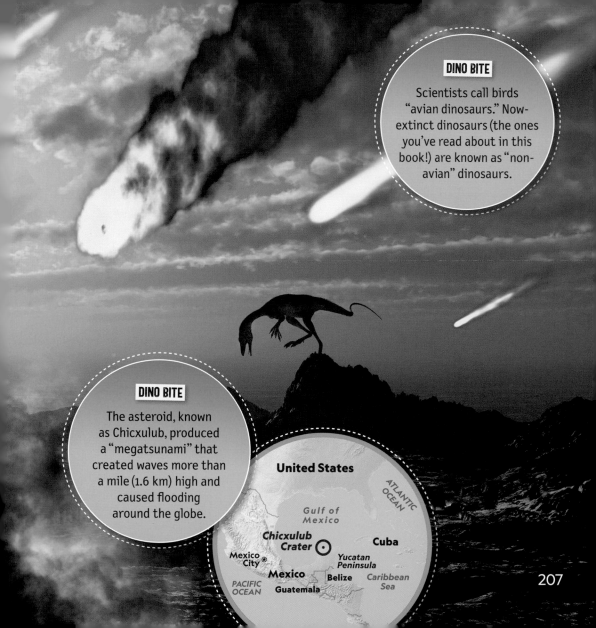

DINO BITE

Scientists call birds "avian dinosaurs." Now-extinct dinosaurs (the ones you've read about in this book!) are known as "non-avian" dinosaurs.

DINO BITE

The asteroid, known as Chicxulub, produced a "megatsunami" that created waves more than a mile (1.6 km) high and caused flooding around the globe.

United States

ATLANTIC OCEAN

Gulf of Mexico

Chicxulub Crater ⊙

Cuba

Mexico City ⊛

Yucatan Peninsula

Mexico

Belize

Caribbean Sea

PACIFIC OCEAN

Guatemala

DINO HIGH
CLASS SUPERLATIVES

Most Likely to Succeed

Dinosaurs were some of the biggest, toughest, most ferocious animals that have ever walked our planet. They ruled Earth for 165 million years. That's more than 500 times as long as humans have existed! Yet even the mightiest dinosaurs didn't last forever. When a space rock the size of a city slammed into the planet with the force of more than a billion atomic bombs, it wiped out all types of dinosaurs ... all except for one. Birds could survive on many different foods, from insects to seeds. Their small bodies didn't need much fuel. And above all, they could fly to new places in their quest for survival. These small feathered dinosaurs may have seemed puny compared to mighty *Tyrannosaurus* and *Triceratops*. But these underdogs came out on top.

YEP— I'M A PRETTY **BIG** DEAL!

Biggest Heavyweight,
pages 28–29

Brainiest, **pages 82–83**

Super Sprinter,
pages 140–141

Class Clown, **pages 152–153**

INDEX

Boldface indicates illustrations.

INDEX
CONTINUED

GLOSSARY

Here are just some of the many dino-related words you'll want to know to hone your Jurassic smarts!

ALLOSAUR – a type of carnivorous dinosaur, usually with a long, narrow skull and small arms that ended in three-fingered hands

ANKYLOSAUR – a type of four-legged, armored dinosaur that was likely an herbivore

CERATOPSIAN – a type of four-legged dinosaur whose large head had horns, a beak, and a bony frill

GONDWANA – a large continent, formed of today's South America, Africa, Antarctica, and Australia, that was believed to have existed in Earth's Southern Hemisphere during the end of the Paleozoic era

MEGALOSAUR – a huge carnivorous dinosaur that lived during the Jurassic and early Cretaceous

ORNITHOPODS – a type of herbivorous dinosaur that likely walked on two legs—although some used the toes on their front limbs to walk on all fours

PACHYCEPHALOSAUR – a type of two-legged dinosaur with a thick skill and a domed or flat head

PANGAEA – a land area that once connected the Northern and Southern Hemispheres from 235 to 200 million years ago

SAUROPOD – a type of large four-legged herbivore with a long neck and tail and a small head

STEGOSAUR – a type of four-legged herbivore with defensive plates along its back

THEROPOD – a type of carnivorous dinosaur that likely moved on two legs

TYRANNOSAUR – a large carnivore that moved on two legs and had a powerful jaw and small arms that ended in two fingers

PHOTO CREDITS

Hoffmeyer/SS; 28 (dinosaur silhouette throughout), Kristi Create/AD; 29, Elenarts/AD; 29 (UP), Franco Tempesta/© NGP; 29 (UP CTR), Daniel Eskridge/AD; 29 (LO CTR), Franco Tempesta/© NGP; 29 (LO), Daniel Eskridge/AD; 30 (background), Midstream/SS; 30, De Agostini Picture Library/GI; 31, Michael Rosskothen/AD; 32, Everett Collection Inc/AL; 33, Daniel Eskridge/AD; 34-35 (snowflakes), Viktoriia/AD; 34-35 (CTR), N. Tamura; 34 (UP), Dr. Thomas Rich, Dr. Patricia Vickers Rich, Martin Kundrat; 34 (LO), Daniel Eskridge/AD; 35, © Franco Tempesta; 36-37, schusterbauer/AD; 36 (map throughout), twenty1studio/SS; 36, Win Nondakowit/AD; 37, Gorodenkoff/AD; 38, Herschel Hoffmeyer/SS; 39, © Franco Tempesta; 40-41, Franco Tempesta/© NGP; 42-43 (background throughout), dynamic/SS; 42, Michael Rosskothen/SS; 43 (UP), Michael Rosskothen/AD; 43 (LO), warpaintcobra/AD; 44, Franco Tempesta/© NGP; 45, Elenarts/AD; 46-47 (cacti), Nataly/AD; 46, © Franco Tempesta; 47 (UP), Arthur Dorety/ST/GI; 47 (LO), warpaintcobra/AD; 48 (LE), Franco Tempesta/© NGP; 48 (menu throughout), graficriver_icons_logo/SS; 48 (LO RT), rufar/AD; 49, Herschel Hoffmeyer/SS; 50, Yuriy Priymak/ST/GI; 51, warpaintcobra/AD; 53, Sergey Krasovskiy; 54-55 (utensils), iukhym_vova/AD; 54-55 (UP), Jingmai O'Connor; 54-55 (LO), Andriy Kananovych/SS; 55, Robert Clark/NGIC; 56, animate4/SC; 57, Franco Tempesta/© NGP; 58 (UP), Mike Hettwer/NGIC; 58 (LO), Kat Keene Hogue/NGIC; 59, Paolo Verzone/NGIC; 60, Sergey Krasovskiy/ST/SC; 61, Daniel Eskridge/SS; 61 (CTR RT), Lawrence M. Witmer, Ph.D/Ohio University; 62-63 (rattle), Yevgen Kravchenko/SS; 62, China News Service/GI; 62-63 (CTR), Danny Ye/SS; 63, Gregory Erickson; 64, Gregory Funston; 65, Franco Tempesta/© NGP; 67, Sergey Krasovskiy/ST/GI; 67 (LO RT), Martin Leber/SS; 68-69, Orla/SS; 70, Jason Brougham; 71, Zhao Chuang/PNSO PTE. Ltd.; 72-73 (stars), t1mon344/AD; 72, Dr. Bo Wang; 73 (UP), Pascal Goetgheluck/SC; 73 (LO), Image courtesy of the Royal Saskatchewan Museum; 74, Laurent Marquez; 75, Sergey Krasovskiy/ST/GI; 76-77 (speech bubbles), mejorana777/AD; 76, Franco Tempesta/© NGP; 77 (UP), Michael Rosskothen/AD; 77 (LO), Herschel Hoffmeyer/AD; 78, Mark P. Witton/SC; 78-79 (CTR), Michael Rosskothen/AD; 79, Mark Hallett/ST/AL; 80, SC; 81, Roger Harris/Science Photo Library/GI; 83 (Class Clown), Franco Tempesta/© NGP; 83 (UP), Elenarts/AD; 83 (UP CTR), Daniel Eskridge/AD; 83 (LO CTR), Franco Tempesta/© NGP; 83 (LO), Daniel Eskridge/AD; 85, Julio Lacerda; 86 (globe), Megarupa/SS; 86 (ammonite), alice-photo/SS; 86 (trilobite), Soft Lighting/SS; 86 (LO), Millard H. Sharp/SC; 87, warpaintcobra/AD; 88, john/AD; 89, Jan Sovak/ST/Media Bakery; 90-91 (bandages), monochromeye/SS; 90 (LE), Millard H. Sharp/SC; 90 (RT), Dra. Penélope Cruzado-Caballero; 91, Reimar/AD; 93, Franco Tempesta/© NGP; 94-95 (photos), Courtesy Steve Brusatte; 94 (filmstrip), bupu/AD; 96, Lou-Foto/AL; 97, Tobias Everke/Agentur Focus/Redux Pictures; 99, Zhao Chuang/PNSO PTE. Ltd.; 100-101 (icons), nikiteev_konstantin/SS; 100-101 (beetles), Martin Qvarnström; 100-101 (LO), Image courtesy of the Royal Saskatchewan Museum; 101 (UP), Karen Chin; 101 (LO), Gedeminas/AD; 103, Raul Lunia/Bridgeman Images; 104-105, Martin Kemp/SS; 105, Natural History Museum, London/Bridgeman Images; 106, PvE/AL; 107, © Franco Tempesta; 108-109 (leaves), Olga.And.Design/SS; 108, N. Tamura; 109 (UP), O. Louis Mazzatenta/NGIC; 109 (CTR), April Neander; 109 (LO), Roman Uchytel; 110, Nattika/SS; 111, Franco Tempesta/© NGP; 112-113, meen_na/AD; 115, James Kuether; 116 (UP), Dr. Darla Zelenitsky; 116 (LO), Lida Xing et al. 2021; 117, James Kuether; 118-119, Catmando/SS; 120-121 (DNA), Ohn Mar/SS; 120, John Sibbick/SC; 121 (UP), Julius Csotonyi; 121 (CTR), Michael

Rosskothen/AD; 121 (LO), Paulo de Oliveira/Minden Pictures; 123, Roger Harris/SC; 124, Daniel Eskridge/AD; 125 (UP), MR1805/iStock/GI; 125 (LO), Mark Garlick/Science Photo Library/GI; 126, Millard H. Sharp/SC; 127, Buena Vista Images/Photodisc/GI; 128-129 (clouds), devitaayu/AD; 128, Michael Rosskothen/AD; 129 (UP), Michael Rosskothen/AD; 129 (CTR), Michael Rosskothen/SS; 129 (LO), Michael Rosskothen/SS; 130, © Franco Tempesta; 131, Franco Tempesta/© NGP; 132-133 (tag), YenSuVec/SS; 132-133 (dinosaur silhouette), Steinar/AD; 132-133 (ferns), guliveris/AD; 132-133 (leaves), Ortis/AD; 132-133 (leaves), Yeti Studio/AD; 132 (UP RT), Catmando/AD; 133 (CTR), Sergey Krasovskiy; 133 (CTR RT), YuRi Photolife/SS; 133 (RT foliage), Kimo/AD; 133 (LO), photosvac/AD; 135, N. Tamura; 136, James Kuether; 137 (UP), Michael Rosskothen/SS; 137 (CTR), Matte FX. Matte FX Inc./NGIC; 137 (LO), Mark Garlick/Science Photo Library/AL; 138-139, Franco Tempesta/© NGP; 141, Daniel Eskridge/AD; 141 (UP), Elenarts/AD; 141 (UP CTR), Franco Tempesta/© NGP; 141 (LO CTR), Franco Tempesta/© NGP; 141 (LO), Daniel Eskridge/AD; 143, Márcio L. Castro; 144-145 (leaves), Olga.And.Design/SS; 144, auntspray/AD; 145 (UP), auntspray/AD; 145 (CTR), Corey Ford/ST/SC; 145 (LO), Richard Bizley/SC; 146-147, John/AD; 146 (tooth), Crazytang/iStock/GI; 146 (foot), Francois Gohier/SC; 146 (leg), Millard H. Sharp/SC; 147, David South/AL; 148, Franco Tempesta/© NGP; 149 (UP), Raul Ramos/Creative Beast Studio; 149 (LO), © Franco Tempesta; 150-151, Franco Tempesta/© NGP; 153, Franco Tempesta/© NGP; 153 (UP), Elenarts/AD; 153 (UP CTR), Franco Tempesta/© NGP; 153 (LO CTR), Daniel Eskridge/AD; 153 (LO), Daniel Eskridge/AD; 154-155, dottedyeti/AD; 156-157, Antonio Penas/ST/SC; 158-159 (palette), ksuksu/AD; 158, GL Archive/AL; 159 (UP), Joe/AD; 159 (LO), Entertainment Pictures/AL; 160-161, Julius Csotonyi; 162, Robert A. Smith; 163, James Kuether; 164, © Franco Tempesta; 165 (UP), E.R. Degginger/AL; 165 (LO), AP Photo/Seth Wenig; 166 (UP), Joshua Steadman for WALTER magazine; 166 (LO), Alison Moyer; 167, Justin Kase Conder/JKase Inc.; 168, Akkharat J./AD; 169, James Kuether; 170-171, Stephen Shaver/AL; 171, Wirestock/AL; 173, Franco Tempesta/© NGP; 174-175 (bone), Zhuko/SS; 174, Pecold/AD; 175 (UP), Mark Garlick/Science Photo Library/AL; 175 (LO), Cory Richards/NGIC; 176 (Brachiosaurus), warpaintcobra/AD; 176 (giraffe), jaroslava V/SS; 177, allvision/AD; 178, warpaintcobra/AD; 179 (UP), Andreas Meyer/AD; 179 (LO), Franco Tempesta/© NGP; 180-181 (tools), josepperianes/AD; 180, Jose Antonio Penas/SC; 181 (UP), Russian Photo/AD; 181 (CTR), knickknack/AD; 181 (LO), thanapun/AD; 182, Scott Smith/Corbis Documentary/GI; 183, Daniel Eskridge/AD; 184-185 (fedora), Viktorija Reuta/SS; 184-185 (tools), josepperianes/AD; 184-185 (palette), ksuksu/AD; 184-185 (footprints), WinWin/AD; 184 (trilobites), Soft Lighting/SS; 185 (LO), Volha Kliukina/AD; 185 (RT), Panupong/AD; 186-187, Michael Rosskothen/AD; 188-189, warpaintcobra/AD; 190-191 (cones), owatta/SS; 190, Denver Museum of Nature & Science; 191 (UP), NASA/Goddard/Rebecca Roth; 191 (LO), Tom Mihalek/Reuters; 193, © Franco Tempesta; 194, Phil Degginger/Carnegie Museum/SC; 195, © Franco Tempesta; 196 (CTR RT), Catmando/SS; 196 (LO RT), Cjchiker/Dreamstime; 197, Elenarts/SS; 198-199, Gina Ferazzi/GI; 199, Jim West/AL; 201, Davide Bonadonna; 202-203, Franco Tempesta/© NGP; 204, Trustees of the Natural History Museum; 205, Daniel Eskridge/AD; 206-207, Mark Stevenson/ST/GI; 207, NG Maps 208, voren1/AD; 209, Daniel Eskridge/AD; 209, Daniel Eskridge/AD; 209 (UP), Elenarts/AD; 209 (UP CTR), 216, Franco Tempesta/© NGP; 209 (LO CTR), Daniel Eskridge/AD; 209 (LO), Franco Tempesta/© NGP; 216, Franco Tempesta/© NGP

NATIONAL GEOGRAPHIC and Yellow Border Design are trademarks of the National Geographic Society, used under license.

Since 1888, the National Geographic Society has funded more than 14,000 research, conservation, education, and storytelling projects around the world. National Geographic Partners distributes a portion of the funds it receives from your purchase to National Geographic Society to support programs including the conservation of animals and their habitats. To learn more, visit natgeo.com/info.

For more information, visit nationalgeographic.com, call 1-877-873-6846, or write to the following address:

National Geographic Partners, LLC
1145 17th Street NW
Washington, DC 20036-4688 U.S.A.

For librarians and teachers: nationalgeographic.com/books/librarians-and-educators

More for kids from National Geographic: natgeokids.com

National Geographic Kids magazine inspires children to explore their world with fun yet educational articles on animals, science, nature, and more. Using fresh story-telling and amazing photography, *Nat Geo Kids* shows kids ages 6 to 14 the fascinating truth about the world—and why they should care. **natgeo.com/subscribe**

For rights or permissions inquiries, please contact National Geographic Books Subsidiary Rights:
bookrights@natgeo.com

Designed by Brett Challos

Trade paperback ISBN: 978-1-4263-7374-9
Reinforced library binding ISBN: 978-1-4263-7580-4

The publisher would like to thank the dino-mite team that put this book together: Kathryn Williams, project editor; Sarah J. Mock, senior photo editor; Danny Meldung, photo editor; Jen Geddes, fact-checker; Alix Inchausti, senior production editor; and David Marvin and Lauren Sciortino, associate designers—and a special thanks to Steve Brusatte for his expert review.

Printed in Hong Kong
23/PPHK/1